RETHINKING MODERNITY

RETHINKING MODERNITY: BETWEEN THE LOCAL AND THE INTERNATIONAL

BY ANTIGONI KATSAKOU

RIBA Publishing

© RIBA Publishing, 2020

Published by RIBA Publishing, 66 Portland Place, London, W1B 1AD

ISBN 9781 85946 879 1

The right of Antigoni Katsakou to be identified as the Author of this Work has been asserted in accordance with the Copyright, Designs and Patents Act 1988 sections 77 and 78.

All rights reserved. No part of this publication may be reproduced, stored in a retrieval system, or transmitted, in any form or by any means, electronic, mechanical, photocopying, recording or otherwise, without prior permission of the copyright owner.

British Library Cataloguing-in-Publication Data
A catalogue record for this book is available from the British Library.

Commissioning Editor: Ginny Mills
Assistant Editor: Clare Holloway
Production: Jane Rogers
Designed and typeset by Fakenham Prepress Solutions
Printed and bound by Page Bros, Norwich
Cover image: Atelier Stéphane Fernandez (photograph by Jean Michel Landecy)

While every effort has been made to check the accuracy and quality of the information given in this publication, neither the Author nor the Publisher accept any responsibility for the subsequent use of this information, for any errors or omissions that it may contain, or for any misunderstandings arising from it.

www.ribapublishing.com

CONTENTS

Acknowledgements		vii
About the author		ix
Foreword by Antonio Millan-Gomez		x
Introduction	Modernity: A small word for such a big world	xv
Chapter 1	Tradition and identity	1
Chapter 2	Modernity and context	21
Chapter 3	Materials and colours	45
Chapter 4	The forbidden wor(l)d: Ornament and decoration in the alternative modern	67
Chapter 5	Geometry and spatial experience	91
Chapter 6	The modern diaspora: Latin America (by Antigoni Katsakou and Iliana Miranda-Zacarias)	111
Chapter 7	Modern diaspora and the British interwar period	137
Afterword		167
Timeline		173
Endnotes		174
Index		185

For Nik and Michael.

ACKNOWLEDGEMENTS

All books are collaborative efforts. I am grateful to the editor Ginny Mills for proposing to write this book, and for thus providing the chance to talk about projects which I am especially passionate about. A book that focuses on local contexts demands 'inside' information and guidance, therefore I feel obligated to friends and colleagues around the world for offering their valuable advice and expertise: Karina Contreras Castellanos, Anna Victória Wanderley Silva de Azevedo, Jorge Anibal Manrique Prieto, Fabio Shoyama, Sung-Taeg Nam, María Cecilia Kesman, Sladjana Markovic and Eveline Galatis. For kindly responding to my queries, I thank Virginia Gutiérrez, Jakub Heciak, Ania Cymer and Ljiljana Blagojević.

For sharing her expertise on Mexican modernity, and for her perceptiveness, special thanks are due to Iliana Miranda-Zacarias. I am particularly grateful to Antonio Millan-Gomez for his insight, instructive comments, and above all for sharing my passion for the topics discussed in the book. For contributing with their feedback along the development of this project, I would like to thank Elisabeth Tostrup, Maria Angélica da Silva, Spyros Kaprinis and Eleni Axioti.

I am indebted to a number of people who actively offered their support by generously providing original material, especially to: Claudio Williams, Bettina Cetto, Carlos Warchavchik, Elisabeth Selmer, Dimitris Konstantinidis, Alexandra Tsoukala, Frøde Larsen, Michalis Souvatzidis, Diane Ghirardo, Alejandro Lapunzina, Luis Carranza and George Makris.

I gratefully acknowledge the generous fund granted by the Society of Architectural Historians Great Britain for covering, in part, the image fees.

I would like to express my gratitude to the editorial / production team and external collaborators of RIBA Publishing, especially Susannah Jayes and Kathryn Glendenning, for their professionalism.

Finally, I would like to thank my husband Nik for offering the encouragement I needed to embark on this laborious task, for his unfailing support, and for his ever so helpful, creative suggestions; our son, Michael, for being such an inspiration; my parents, Stamatis and Dina, and my sisters, Dimitra and Sofia, for their unconditional love that lasts beyond time and makes all things possible.

ABOUT THE AUTHOR

Antigoni Katsakou is a London-based architect (ARB) and author, holding a PhD in History and Theory of Architecture from the Swiss Federal Institute of Technology Lausanne (EPFL, 2011). A graduate of the National Technical University of Athens (NTUA, Dipl Arch Eng 1999), of Barcelona Tech (UPC, MArch 2001), and a Visiting Postdoctoral Fellow at the Bartlett School of Graduate Studies (2012-2013) she has been awarded with various funding grants. She has practiced and taught in the UK, Switzerland and Greece; she has presented her scholarly work worldwide and has published in several languages, including the books *The Competition Grid* (RIBA Publishing, 2018) and *Concevoir des logements* (PPUR, 2008).

FOREWORD

There is a challenge that many gifted criticists face at a crucial moment of their career: out of the existing introductions to modern architecture, those that we remember have a special taint that makes them distinctive. And, as different architectural approaches appear with time, new viewpoints are needed. In *Rethinking Modernity: Between the Local and the International*, a straightforward approach is evident as soon as one opens the book or looks at the title. Discussing projects both familiar and little-known in order to demonstrate the concepts in question, this book is a vivid commentary and celebration of architecture that keeps the reader's interest undiminished. This is not a *revision* of, or a search for yet another *definition* of modernity, but a *rethinking* of it, with all the implications such an approach entails.

Criticists of modern architecture are aware of both the bias produced in its development and the plurality of its roots.[1] Paul Ricœur had already pondered a paradox as early as 1961: 'how to become modern and to return to sources, how to revive an old, dormant civilization and take part in universal civilization'.[2] This was a point that fostered Kenneth Frampton's *Critical Regionalism*: 'regional or national cultures must today, more than ever, be ultimately constituted as locally inflected manifestations of "world culture"'.[3] Frampton provided in six pragmatic points an accurate representation of the situation at the time and stressed oppositions between different attitudes (Regionalism of Restriction as opposed to Regionalism of Liberation). Critiques of functionalism and facilitation of communications served the study of traditions and the renewal of cultural knowledge while promoting individual identities and establishing a social solidarity of a new kind.

When, in 1978, Alan Colquhoun distinguished between *form* and *figure*, a new understanding of the modern could already be sensed amongst scholars that sought a sounder interpretation of architectural practice. Colquhoun understood that the dualism *form/function* could no longer provide the required insight to explain the break from older cultures and traditions. He proposed the dialectic of *form* and *figure* instead, with *form* perceived as a configuration related to no particular meaning, whereas *figure* is perceived as inseparable from the specific culture within which designers work and is shaped by recognisable elements. Associative meanings helped renew architectural practice, not by what existed before 'but by emergent social and technological facts, operating on a minimum number of constant physiological and psychological laws.'[4]

Critiques of functionalism and facilitation of communications served the study of traditions and the renewal of cultural knowledge, while promoting individual identities and establishing a social solidarity of a new kind. Thirty years later, these dynamic views have spread across the planet, with all the resulting difficulties and contingencies. The author is clear in the Conclusion about the extent of such a state of affairs: today, we must encompass all cases with enough paradigmatic strength to propose entirely new readings.

Sufficient time has elapsed to suggest new interpretations of the original concepts. New classifications of architectural modernity are being considered because the corpus of works produced after criticists and historians coined the term 'postmodern' (with similar bluntness to the transformers of modernity into an International Style) is more than impressive. Modern and postmodern can now be understood as differentiated positions in the century-long struggle between art and technology rather than as chronological eras. At the same time, a higher degree of precision has been proposed in respect to terms used to describe relative phenomena, offering a fascinating challenge to re-discover past and present architecture and propose future classifications.[5]

Nevertheless, there was one clear aspect in the debate induced by the postmodern: if we continue labouring defective assumptions, we are bound to reproduce them, with added risks. Mis-readings of original concepts appear now at a global scale and silence can be cruel in our mass-media age, where a lack of headlines on a project can be mistaken as irrelevance.

The appeal of *Rethinking Modernity* lies in its much needed critical courage. One is relieved to see included great works by modest designers, while low-key interventions are also recovered from neglect, finding new life. Accordingly, architectural modernity is treated as a phenomenon that went beyond the avant-garde, to consider outstanding 'silent' Nordic, Mediterranean or Iberian-American architects, and even Far-Eastern examples, quite often forgotten.

As is evident from the chapter headings, rethinking is developed, stressing new sets of architectural values that must be applied to modernity as we understand it today. Since original undertakings have to do with a concern for origins or *arché* [αρχή] (beginning of things), Antigoni Katsakou reminds us that *tradition and identity are inseparable*, and that architectural quality can be approached today as inextricably twined with subjective, haptic spatial experiences rejoiced by users. She thus provides analytical strategies that are considerate to both forerunners and recent descendants, and which are necessary to understand continuity on the one hand and the ever-changing nature of architectural creativity on the other. These reflections come to light at the precise moment when the centenary of several avant-garde masters is celebrated. They did not ignore *spontaneous* architecture or *archaic* cultures; rather, they learnt from them, preceding the pragmatic links between so-called Critical Regionalism and local cultures.

There is neither understanding nor representation without interpretation, and interpretation often relies on normative qualities that prove their usefulness in critical reflection. The criticist then becomes in turn subject to the norm as any other member of the community, a fact very seldom interiorised. In this sense, the author displays an unassuming turn of mind, taking care not to hasten to conclusions.

This is a book to reflect upon, but also a book to enjoy truly great architecture, without pretensions, through the presentation of facts and their sheer beauty, autonomy and actuality. *Rethinking Modernity* is a breath of fresh air for designers willing to broaden their scope and a testimony of good intentions towards young architects-to-be.

Antonio Millan-Gomez, Architect COAC, PhD
Professor of Architectural Representation at Barcelona TECH (UPC)

INTRODUCTION

MODERNITY: A SMALL WORD FOR SUCH A BIG WORLD

For a long time, the modern in architecture has been identified with the work of an avant-garde originating from central Europe and the USA. It was not until the post-war period, particularly during the 1970s, that an alternative concerned with different corners of the world and lesser-known architects became the object of systematic study. This book deals with this alternative modern, casting a closer look at the concepts and design tools that engendered it, through the work, especially during the period between the two world wars, of relevant architects who have been particularly influential within the context of modernity, in both national and local contexts.

Modernity is used here as a general term, describing the social and cultural context defined by the process of modernisation, which intensified at the end of the 19th and beginning of the 20th centuries. For most historians, modernity coincides with a rupture with past traditions and styles. Discussing the relationship between modernity and architecture, the architectural theorist Hilde Heynen refers to modernism as one of the effects of this rupture, and as 'the body of artistic and intellectual ideas and movements that deal with the process of modernization and with the experience of modernity'.[1] Although modernism has been established as a term encompassing various interpretations of the modern, departing from the original, purist canon, in this book it is mostly substituted by the concept of modernity. This is done intentionally as, in architecture at least, modernism still seems to imply a superiority of the modern, grasped essentially in terms of the work of the avant-garde, the mainstream, the 'canon'.[2]

Historical texts that have been significant for long-standing, collective perceptions of modern architecture, such as Henry-Russell Hitchcock and Philip Johnson's *The International Style* (1932), Nikolaus Pevsner's *Pioneers of the Modern Movement* (1936) or Sigfried Giedion's *Space, Time and Architecture* (1941),[3] were almost contemporary with the architecture they were tackling. Being part of this history-in-the-making, they sought to consolidate rather than expand, to focus rather than enlarge the concept of the modern movement in order to affirm its cohesion. They thus heavily contributed to the formulation of stereotypes that identified, especially during the post-war period, internationality with uniformity, regularity with monotony, and objectivity with loss of humanity.

Hitchcock and Johnson focused on the USA, Germany, France and Holland. Already based in Britain at the time of his book's publication, Pevsner traced a lineage between William Morris and his compatriot Walter Gropius; the trail of important architectural events at the end of his book contextualised the modern in England, Germany and Austria, the USA, France, Belgium and Holland. Giedion remained within the same geographical boundaries; Frank Lloyd Wright, Adolf Loos, Walter Gropius, Le Corbusier, Mies van der Rohe and Alvar Aalto became identified with the genesis of a New Tradition in architecture.

At the same time, the concept of the modern as a global, 'international' phenomenon was inherent in most of the texts heralding its existence, whether in the manifestos of the masters or the texts of historians and theorists. However, it was also clear that the global reach of the modern should answer to a set of formal, functional and ethical rules explicitly stated in or inferred from specific versions of history. These design properties, which encompassed a breach with historical styles and were materialised in the use of flat roofs, of purist volumes in asymmetrical compositions, of large glazed surfaces and of building structures in metal and concrete, identified the 'canon'.

In a way, the CIAM (Congrès Internationaux d'Architecture Moderne), the official voice of the modern movement and an organisation to which Giedion served as secretary, was typical of this essentially 'contained' approach that marked the beginnings of the movement. The idea of representatives from different countries and parts of the world was inherent in the CIAM, which was at least bilingual from the very beginning; however, participation from outside Europe and North America was not actively sought until the 1940s. The declaration of the first CIAM was signed by more than 20 architects originating from eight different countries; still, all of them were located in western and central Europe (with a Swiss predominance among the signing members).[4]

The CIAM was launched in 1928 and came to an end in 1959, when the 'modern', especially its functionalist, urban-planning principles, was heavily criticised by architects such as Peter and Alison Smithson and Jacob Bakema (Team X). Nevertheless, more recent versions of architectural history have clearly identified its relevance even for our contemporary production of architecture. Giedion's fifth edition of *Space, Time and Architecture* (1967) encompassed the modern's Third Generation, and architects such as Jørn Utzon, José Luis Sert, Kenzo Tange and Fumihiko Maki. Thus, he expanded the list of 'masters' as well as the geographical boundaries of reference.

The problem of interpretation did not merely concern the geographical range of projects that could be classified as 'modern'. Most importantly, it had to do with the cultural and formal paradigms able to expand the understanding of the modern and explain its varied expressions across the globe. After World War II, Bruno Zevi delivered a new interpretation of the modern by tying up the notion of its future evolution with its organic lineage, and the aspiration to a democratic society with the dynamic unravelling of the architectural space. Theorists such as Manfredo Tafuri engaged in a 'derogative' approach, questioning the modern movement and seeking 'to establish the theoretical foundations of a different architecture.'[5]

Beyond theoretical stances of history, inextricably linked with views about what architecture is or ought to be, Kenneth Frampton's *Modern Architecture: A Critical History* (1980)[6] emphasised the fact that the modern was not a question of stereotypical applications of a mainstream, but of rich and diversified manifestations of it across the globe. This interpretation opened the door to a list of -isms, of the kind of modern regionalism or regional modernism;[7] it was a way of interpreting this diversity under the umbrella of what has already been established as one single, modern movement. Frampton presented critical regionalism as 'a decentralised mode of cultural resistance,'[8] and featured projects from Portugal, Spain, Italy, Greece, Denmark, Mexico and Japan. In his *Genealogy of Modern Architecture* (2015), he established three conflicting cultural paradigms constantly in interaction throughout the evolution of the modern movement (contemporary era included), the technological, the classical and the vernacular, and 'a hybrid species of vernacular modernism' that 'may be identified in modern architecture from 1923 onwards.'[9]

The question of modern 'genotypes' remains predominant in the present era, within an architectural context that continues to develop after at least two, viable paradigms rooted in the tradition of the modern: the technological paradigm, which attempts to keep up to speed with advanced techno-scientific methods and a digitised era of design, and the paradigm of formal renovation. Projects that belong to the first category are often less focused on the social or cultural meaning that the building holds. They are frequently conceived by processes of mimesis of the natural world in art, which were popular in historical periods before the modern. This approach is opposed to the second category that mainly relies on abstraction in order to interpret the physical world. Although the paradigm of a linear progress in history, propelled by technological achievements and inexhaustible physical resources, has long been eclipsed, the ideal of a social mission in architecture remains valid in questions of sustainability and of a rational use of the world's natural resources. It seems today that the modern constitutes a live tradition, which feeds from broad interpretations. For this reason, design strands that drew on the heritage and economy of means characterising regional cultures and that were the way forward for a distinct, alternative lineage of the modern remain particularly relevant, as well as still largely unexplored.

Thus, most of the architects discussed in this book make part of the modern that has been described as 'vernacular', 'local' or even 'national'. They have also been discussed as 'half moderns', a term both pejorative and wanting, undermining these projects' artistic and cultural integrity, which is often more solidly rooted in conceptual terms than mere transpositions of aesthetic rules. The architects here are often considered the 'silent' or 'neglected' figures of the modern, attracting little interest from the international press until the 1970s or 1980s. Their place of origin, on the periphery of Europe and the USA, and the relatively local impact of their architectural production contributed to this attitude. This book also aims to rethink modernity by juxtaposing these projects with works of the well-known masters in order to challenge what has been considered as canonical. Contradictions inherent in the work of the pioneers make the direct connection of the alternative with the mainstream apparent, and accentuate the importance that alternative analytical gazes hold for an expanded interpretation of the modern.

It is impossible to talk of a 'localised' (or a 'vernacular') modern, or of a 'specific' modernity and not refer to countries of the Mediterranean basin or of Latin

America.[10] These parts of the world proved quite resilient to a-local, flattening building concepts. The fear of being culturally assimilated by the sovereign powers of their broader regions worked as a motivation for unique and particularly fertile transformations of the mainstream modern. Thus, emphasis is placed here on these parts, with which the alternative modern is inevitably associated, as well as with ulterior, post-war transformations of the work of avant-garde masters, such as Le Corbusier. Additionally, countries of the Mediterranean are scarcely looked at in parallel with Latin America, despite an apparent kinship, sporadically acknowledged in publications focusing on one of them, or on specific representatives of modernity in these two contexts. Nevertheless, these areas remain only a small part of the alternative modern.

The alternative modern developed through frictions between local cultural contexts, construction processes, materials and building types, and the intent to assume an international spirit in art and design. The term was introduced by Valerie Fraser to describe the adaptations of the European mainstream by Latin American architects, through a closely knit dialogue with the building context, understood in terms of the natural landscape or of existing (popular or monumental) constructions, with local lifestyles and climates, as well as through the use of local materials, techniques, works of art or indigenous flora, regional colours and textures.[11]

This book follows this approach thematically, exploring the basic components of the architectural design in relation to alternative modernity. Thus, the first two chapters tackle tradition, identity and context as priority conceptual parameters; the next two chapters look at materials, colours and ornamentation as the means for materialising it; the fifth chapter deals with the built outcome and spatial experience as a direct result of a design approach centred around the individual user, instead of on collective considerations. The last two chapters offer the opportunity to examine the mainstream in a direct parallel with examples of alternative modernity, through the work of the diaspora and of architects who have been equally exposed both to the local and the international dimension of the modern. In most chapters, a sub-theme organises the examples studied: the Mediterranean patio house, integration into the land's contour, the intrinsic relation between materials and colours and the way it has been publicised in modernity, muralism and the visual impact of asymmetrical spatial sequences.

The book also seeks to explore the affinities between the trajectories of selected architectural figures and the intricate ways in which architects and projects often seem to be linked across remote parts of the world. Within modernity, one man's teacher has been another man's trainee, while ideas were sometimes circulated surprisingly fast and straightforwardly. Thus, discussion sometimes returns to individual architects and their trajectories on different occasions and in more than one chapter; all pieces of information aim to tell their story in a relatively thorough way. Examples draw mostly on a medium-size building scale and often cover single-family houses, as these became essentially the icons of modernity around the world.

The focus of this book is on the interwar period. The two decades between the two world wars are particularly interesting for the dissemination of the modern, not least because of the social and financial circumstances presiding over a large part of the world. The 1920s have been described as a consolidation period of the modern, since a large enough number of projects and theoretical works had by then been produced to enable talk of an 'internationally valid' architectural trend.[12] By the next decade, these works were being broadly disseminated around the world. Equally, the interwar period provides an opportunity to observe the articulation of alternative expressions of modernity early enough as to pinpoint their existence as integral strands of the modern, and not as accessory tropes of it. In some cases, post-war projects are also considered because of their explicit connection with the topics examined.

The book aims at a better understanding of an architectural precedent that is still very much alive today. Included in the following discussions are a few contemporary examples meant to demonstrate this continuity. The following study intends to demonstrate modernity as a rich and lastingly exciting array of concepts that allude to sequences, and as a multi-layered, constantly reinvigorated tradition of syntheses, rather than that of ruptures and partitions.

… CHAPTER 1

TRADITION AND IDENTITY

Examining the work of the Italian-originated Brazilian architect Lina Bo Bardi, Josep Maria Montaner wrote of two kinds of modernity: the 'universal' modernity and a 'specific' one, under which he 'classifies' Bo Bardi.[1] By 'universal' modernity, he describes an international architecture that has been systematically promoted through various types of media. By 'specific' modernity, he defines architectural work that gradually achieves its value as a universal work of art through the symbiosis in its body of both an international modernity and a local culture. One can also safely assume that this second kind of modernity takes relatively longer to become 'discovered' on a global level.

The international, a-local approach of the New Architecture, as opposed to the question of local identities, has been a constant point of strain for a large part of modernity, in many different contexts. This tension primarily stemmed from a breach with the past that needed to be both symbolic and literal. For the new architecture to pinpoint its innovative character and cohesion, it was essential to clash with the past, especially with the immediate, eclectic past which was deemed inefficient for the needs of the modern man and industrialisation. The breach with the past could not be straightforwardly materialised in countries that were still in the process of affirming their national integrity, and within which eclecticism has hardly had the leverage it acquired in central and northern Europe.

The focus of this chapter is mainly on architectural work concerned with the context of the project, specifically as a means of reaffirming a local identity and an 'identity-specific' modernity. Local identity here refers to a unique set of traits corresponding to a specific group of people, inherent of their cultural and artistic production through many years. The character and cultural identity of a place and its folk are identified in the existing built environment, in its body of vernacular architecture and what is understood as tradition in various fields of this people's creative activity during different periods of time. By using as a starting point the building typology of the Mediterranean patio house, this chapter discusses different notions of the concept of 'tradition'. It also looks at the ways in which they have been grasped as synonyms of local identity; all this, in a period where the modern movement was being widely disseminated as the predominant building expression of a new machinist era.

In countries with such a long cultural heritage as Greece and Italy, tradition was dually grasped in the beginning of the 20th century in relation both to a relatively recent past, corresponding to the vernacular (understood as an expression of popular/naïve art, in the sense of an 'architecture without architects'[2]), and a remote one, corresponding to the classical antiquity of ancient Greece or Rome. In fact, there was even choice as to how remote this 'classical' past could be. In Greece, architects such as Dimitris Pikionis were investigating both the antiquity and the vernacular. Others, such as Aristotelis Zachos, focused on the country's Byzantine past while at the same time promoting the popular culture of the last century. In Brazil, where the presence of past traditions was not so dominant, partly because of an extraordinarily broad range of cultures, the search for Brazilian-ness in the first decades of the 20th century equally involved different notions of the past and artistic avant-garde groups.[3] On the one hand, the Antropófagos of Oswald de Andrade looked at Brazil's precolonial past; on the other, Lúcio Costa promoted a unique notion of national heritage based on the Barroco Mineiro (the 18th-century Baroque of the mining society of Minas Gerais), seeking to 'construct' a continuity between Brazil's past and the teachings of Le Corbusier, while at the same time fighting the established French academicism.[4]

In the quest to assert, study and preserve the unique characteristics of local artistic production, a predominant role was played by language, climate, landscape and lifestyle. They were, in fact, perceived as abridging values between the classical past and the vernacular. The Mediterranean patio house held a central position in this research axis, as belonging both to the classical antiquity and the anonymous architecture of the folk. At the same time, it embodied the ideal of a simple way of life, developed in harmony with nature and the users' needs, and based on the economy of means, both material and aesthetic, a concept close to modern ideas of construction.

LA CASA ALL'ITALIANA
In Italy, both the classical approach of the Novecento movement (counting amid its members the painters Giorgio de Chirico, Carlo Carrà and Mario Sironi), and of Marinetti's and Sant'Elia's futurism, and more radical rationalists (most

representative of whom were the Gruppo 7) sought to appropriate the vernacular. Among the publications where the questions of Mediterraneitá and Italianeitá were being debated was the design magazine *Domus*, launched by Gio Ponti in 1928. Ponti is an architect whose name is closely connected with the search for an Italian identity (essentially through his concept of the Italian house). A modern paradigm of the Universal Man, throughout the years of his professional activity he remained active not only in architecture but also in publishing, furniture and clothing design, painting and ceramics.

The first issue of *Domus* was characteristically launched under the title *Architettura ed arredamento dell'abitazione moderna in cittá ed in campagna* ('Architecture and furnishing of the modern house in the town and the countryside'). It contained Ponti's ideas on an Italian-styled house (casa all'italiana):[5]

> *An Italian style house is not the padded and fitted shelter of those who have to protect themselves from a rough climate. ... The Italian house is the place we have chosen to enjoy our life in, where we happily possess the beauties given us for long seasons by our land and our sky.*[6]

Ponti explored the ways in which a house may organically flow, harmonically connecting the indoors with the outdoors and with its natural setting, in a number of projects along his professional career. Most of them were published in *Domus*, side to side with proposals focusing on the 'modernisation' of the residential unit, an example of which is Luigi Figini and Gino Pollini's Casa Elettrica of 1930.[7] (Figini and Pollini were two of the founders of the Gruppo 7.)

Ponti's project for a Villa alla Pompeiana (Figure 1.1; published in *Domus* in 1934) is directly evocative of Italy's antiquity, while through the choice of materials it is resonant of his country's popular architecture.[8] The villa (which was never built) is presented as a weekend refuge from the speedy rhythms of the modern city and its spaces are arranged around a courtyard in a square layout, entirely open on one side to the surroundings. Developed on a single level, the villa features three single-pitched aisles, following a rationalist, tripartite logic which Ponti frequently used in his subsequent work: the guest rooms, along with the rest of the private

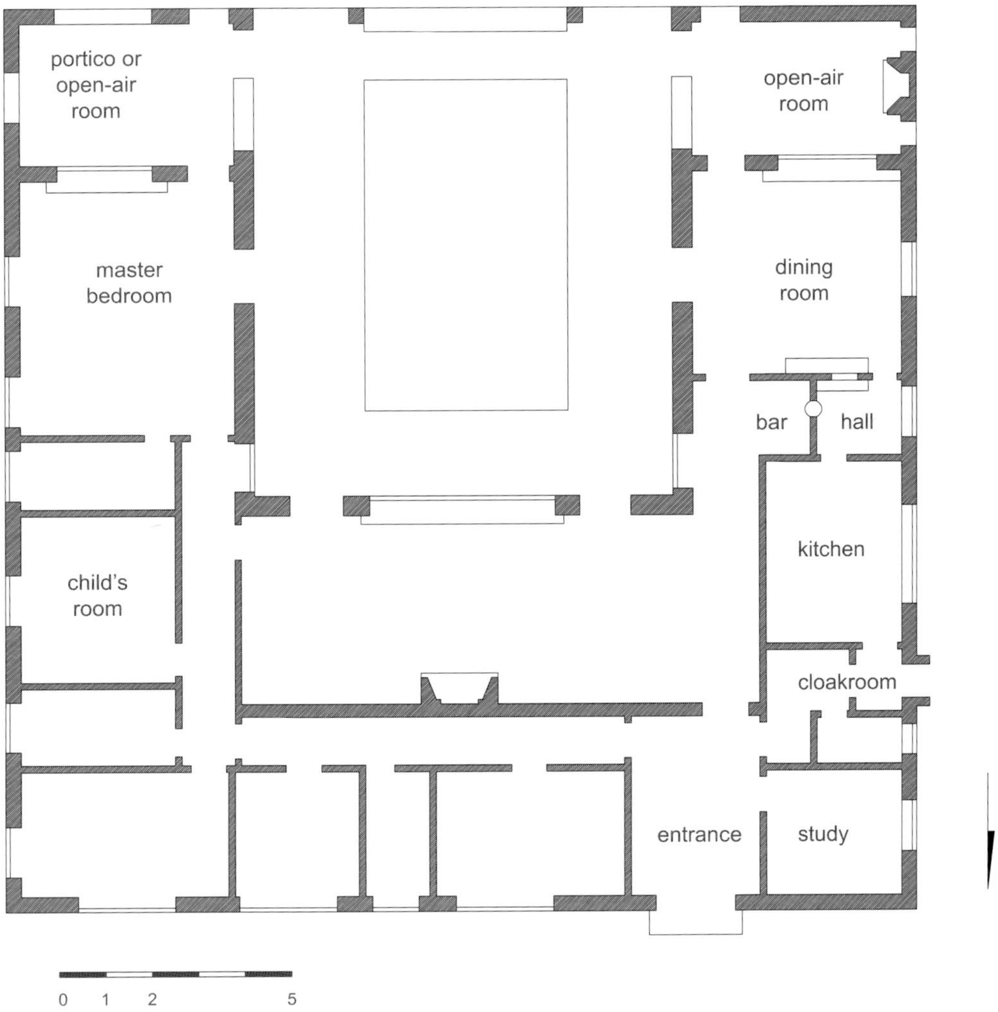

FIGURE 1.1 Plan of Gio Ponti's Pompeiian-style villa, 1934.

spaces, are grouped into a night-time zone occupying the eastern aisle, while services and daytime spaces are set up in the two remaining sections of the house. The lateral aisles terminate in 'open-air' rooms ('porticos') directly facing south; thus, the house's orientation closely follows the modern standards for sanitary accommodation.

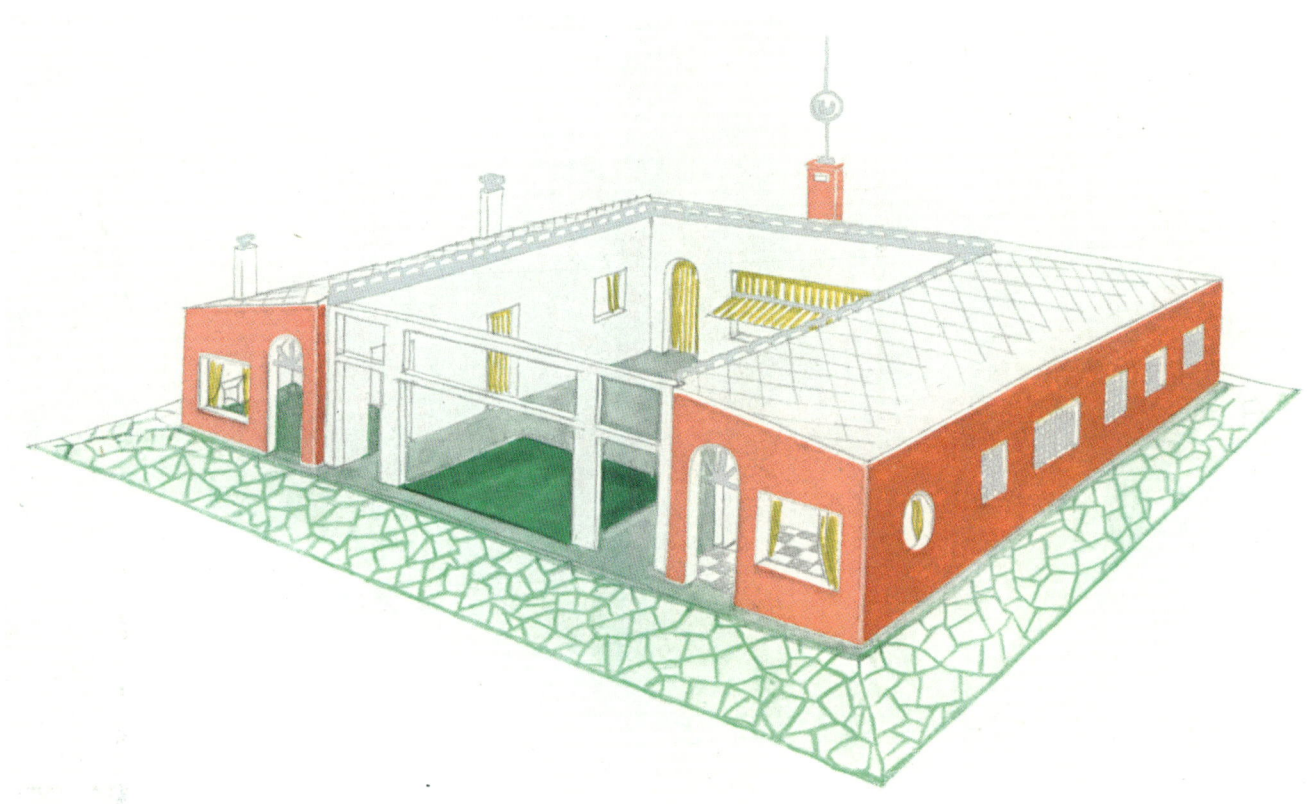

FIGURE 1.2 Perspective drawing of Ponti's Pompeiian-style villa.

Ponti underlines the importance of the house's walls and the way they create a link (instead of a limit) between the enclosed space and nature, '*fan paesaggio*' ('create landscape'). Walls gradually dissolve the interior spaces into the exterior through design devices typical of a regional building culture, such as porticos or the central patio (Figure 1.2). This patio remains an entirely open space or can become a semi-covered one, with the addition of a light, provisional awning: 'Therefore, not abstract, independent architecture, which ends where the walls end: sun, sky, trees, earth, meadows, water, rocks should be composed with the walls, in conciliatory rhythms.'[9]

Equally, Ponti insisted on the choice of materials and their chromatic coordination: the façades are plain, pierced by large square or horizontally elongated openings, and are covered in red stucco, contrasting with the white stucco and polished travertine of the patio walls. Modern materials, such as the linoleum proposed for the flooring of the more private rooms, are combined with Italian marbles, of grey or white colour, used for paving the patio and other construction details.

Thus, Ponti distanced himself from the way the Mediterranean was grasped by many architects of the modern. The geometric qualities and monochromatic volumes typical of the islands of the Aegean Sea or of the Capri Gulf married well with the abstract principles of the modern.[10] Ponti also explored this tradition with the help of the Austrian architect Bernard Rudofsky,[11] but it is not its formal properties that he sought to reproduce. Instead, he pursued primarily a lifestyle rooted in the place's climate and its natural, unaffected features. The theme of the central patio is a recurrent one in his mature work (such as villas Arreaza and Nemazee). For Ponti, a project is born from the ground and modelled to harmonise with the land's contour. Anchored to its surroundings, it is adapted to the standards of modern dwellings but can never be conceived in detachment from its geographical context. Because of such characteristics, a house is also meant to provide a chance for serenity and refocusing on one's self amid the frantic nature of modern life.

THE MAN-MADE AND THE LINES OF THE GREEK LANDSCAPE

The ideal of a perfect symbiosis between the natural and the man-made is also an essential conceptual component of the architecture of Dimitris Pikionis (1887–1968), a contemporary of Ponti's in neighbouring Greece. Pikionis is mostly known internationally for his post-World War II landscape project of the pathways up the Acropolis and Philopappou hills. But his quest for a unique Hellenic identity started as early as 1912; he explored both the Greek vernacular and the country's classical past. After completing his basic studies in civil engineering in Athens in 1908,[12] and staying abroad (in Munich and Paris) for three years, Pikionis returned to Greece to start his professional activity. His friendship with de Chirico and acquaintance with his metaphysical painting theory, as well as his enthusiasm for Paul Cézanne's Cubist technique of representing space and nature, were two significant sources of inspiration from his stay abroad.

FIGURE 1.3 Dimitris Pikionis, study photograph of the Rodakis House, Aegina, photographed in 1912.

While testing his hand in painting the countryside around Athens, Pikionis took part in the movement of 'return to the roots', which placed emphasis on cultural heritage and the qualities of the Hellenic landscape. He became a founding member of the Association for the Study of Greek Popular Art, one of the primary goals of which was to gather and safeguard artistic artefacts from all over the country. He studied the Rodakis House (c. 1880; Figure 1.3) on the island of Aegina, where the neoclassical tradition of the formal architecture of the island's capital settlement coexisted with the architecture of the everyday.[13] The house was built in the interior of the island by a local farmer for his own use. Two of Pikionis' painter friends, Klaus Vrieslander and Julio Kaimi, declared it to be a 'great work of art',[14] whose form generated from and thus perfectly blended with the Greek landscape. Although their praise concerned mostly the simple and spontaneous expression of the owner's craftsmanship (equally manifest in the symbolic elements of naïve ornamentation employed in the house's façades), Pikionis' latter work proves that the house's plain, cubic forms, well thought-out proportions and simple and functional plan were for him equally influential.

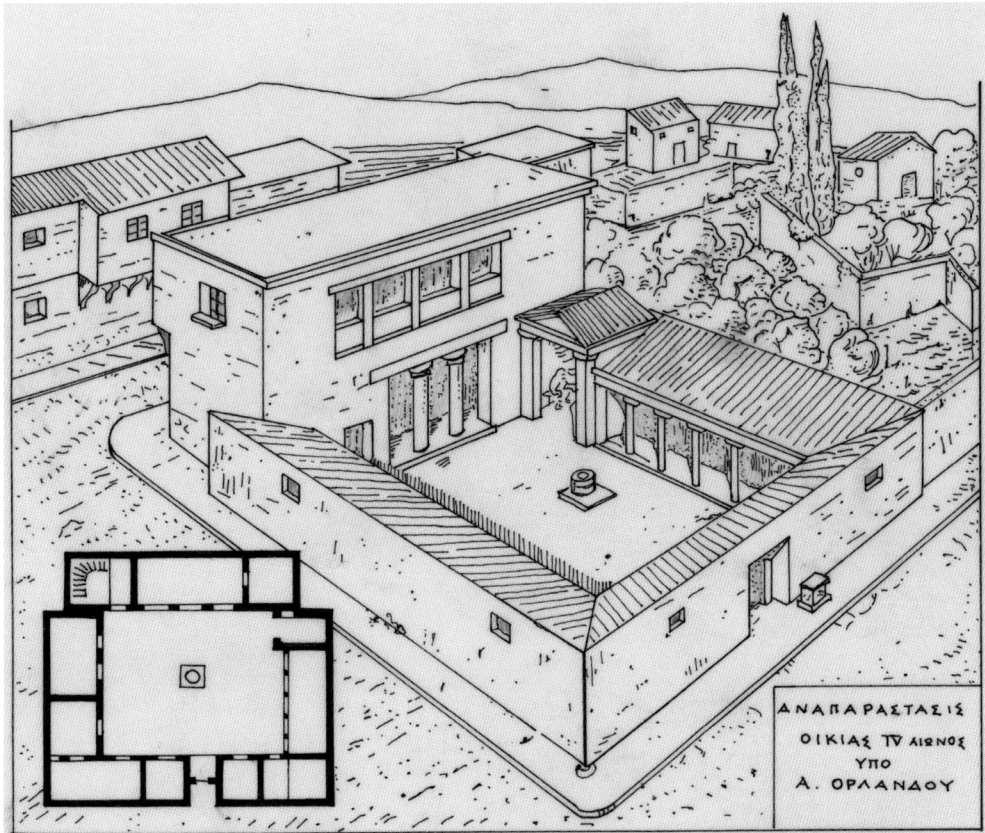

FIGURE 1.4 Drawing of the fourth-century Priene Villa by Anastassios Orlandos, which was used by Dimitris Pikionis as inspiration for the Karamanos residence.

In 1925, Pikionis tackled again the theme of the courtyard house, in the Karamanos brothers' residence that he built in Athens (sadly, now demolished). This time, inspiration came from the plans of a Hellenistic villa at Priene (Figure 1.4), published by his colleague at the National Technical University of Athens, Anastassios Orlandos. The spaces of the Priene Villa are arranged around a central courtyard, on a single level, except for the back, which extends onto a second floor. Pikionis wrote about the villa: 'The square windows, the oblong openings serving as supports and lintels, the absence of a cornice – all these devices were loosely related to contemporary architectural solutions, but they were also to be found in our own popular tradition.'[15]

FIGURE 1.5 Dimitris Pikionis, Karamanos residence, Athens, external view, 1925.

In the Karamanos residence (Figures 1.5 and 1.6), the small courtyard at the back of the house condensed living, sleeping and services along its sides, in the way the high stone wall bordering the courtyard in the Rodakis House encompassed the necessities of everyday life. Pikionis commented on the Karamanos residence's flat roof (as opposed to the single-sloped roof of the Priene Villa) and the square openings of the building's plain, unornamented façades. He explained that he opted for these, 'ignorant of similar preferences expressed by architects of the New Art in other parts of the world', thus endorsing for the first time the principles of the New Architecture, 'by way of his own personal reasons'.[16] Indeed, the photos of the finished project speak of the rationalist logic of its volumetric composition and the austerity of its morphological expression. They appear in stark contrast with the most frequently published drawings of the Karamanos residence, where the Hellenistic paradigm emerges amid an abundant vegetation, in a depiction close to 19th-century Romantic paintings of antique ruins, inspired by the theories of Ruskin.[17]

FIGURE 1.6 Dimitris Pikionis, Karamanos residence, elevation with view to Irakliou Street, 1925.

TRADITION AND IDENTITY

Pikionis explained later in his career the reasons that the modern movement was well received by many Greek architects during the 1920s and 1930s:

> *If the more perceptive minds among us accepted and embraced the Modern Movement at that time, it was for the following reasons: it promised to become the embodiment of organic truth; it was austere, and fundamentally simple; it was governed by a geometry that conveyed a universal design capable of symbolising our age.*[18]

He produced his work that is closest to modern principles in the beginning of the 1930s, when he designed the Pefkakia Primary School in Athens (Figure 1.7). The school was part of a building programme promoted by the liberal government of Eleftherios Venizelos (1928–33), which planned the construction of 4,000 school buildings, almost three times more than had been built since Greece gained independence in 1821.[19] The task was mainly entrusted to a new generation of architects, either recently graduated from the School of Architecture of the National Technical University of Athens or returning to Greece after studying in architectural schools in Germany or France: Mitsakis (a personal friend of Pikionis), Valentis, Panayotakos and the CIAM members Despotopoulos, Karantinos and Papadakis. Most of them eagerly supported the functionalist ideals of this period.

Although faithfully following these principles, Pikionis' school highlights the architect's priority for merging the natural and man-made qualities of the place, by perfectly adapting to the land's steep contour. The main building stands on the plot's highest point, while the six classrooms, distributed on either side of it, are arranged as platforms with individual entrances, and each with its own outdoor space, around the school's main courtyard, itself developed in three separate levels. Ferlenga talks of the project's Loosian qualities, in the way the distinctly distinguished functions of the school are articulated in separate volumes and levels.[20] Nevertheless, Pikionis noted, 'As soon as it was completed, I found it did not satisfy me. It occurred to me then that the universal spirit had to be coupled with the spirit of nationhood.'[21] From this point onward, he changed course, striving in his work for the perfect synthesis of the contemporary and the international with the local and the specific. A perfect congruity between the light, the air and the

FIGURE 1.7 Dimitris Pikionis, Pefkakia Primary School, Lycabettus hill, Athens, 1931, northwestern elevation.

land's geometry[22] is the basis of Pikionis' transcendental architecture of his mature post-World War II production.

THE ESSENCE OF MEXICO

The charm of the Mediterranean and its traditional buildings was not limited to its neighbouring countries, even in this period of new artistic ventures. On the other side of the Atlantic, Mexico can offer a similar story of an architect who could as easily as Pikionis be described as an 'anomaly figure in the panorama of modern architecture'.[23]

Luis Barragán (1902–88) is probably best known internationally for his accomplishments in landscape design, through his seminal work of the Pedregal housing development (*see* pages 99–100) in the south of Mexico City; however, he also displays a similarity with Pikionis (Figure 1.8) in an array of themes in his architectural trajectory. For Barragán, Mediterranean inspiration came from North

FIGURE 1.8 Dimitris Pikionis, the Rodakis House, 1912, study of the winepress façade.

Africa and the Arab vernacular that he recognised from his travels to the Alhambra in Granada, Spain. In the privacy and serenity of the Muslim gardens, Barragán identified the qualities of the traditional *Tapatío* gardens of his home city of Guadalajara, in Mexico, where he spent the first years of his career; in the gardens' surrounding walls, which offered enclosure and privacy, he recognised the lifestyle of the colonial haciendas;[24] in the volumetric harmony of the flat roofs and the unadorned cubes of varied heights he saw the architecture of Mexican villages.

Upon finishing his studies in 1924, Barragán travelled for the first time in Europe. In Paris, he visited the Exposition des Arts Décoratifs, where Le Corbusier was exhibiting his Pavillon de l'Esprit Nouveau. Barragán was already familiar with the teachings of Le Corbusier and of Bauhaus, from his years at the Escuela Libre de Ingenieros in Guadalajara and through magazine articles and books. But at the Exposition des Arts Décoratifs it was Ferdinand Bac's allegoric reproductions of Arab gardens that mostly impressed him.[25]

On his return to Guadalajara, Barragán brought back with him copies of at least two of Bac's illustrated stories, *Les Jardins Enchantés* (Figure 1.9) and *Les Colombières*, and started working on a series of houses, where the influence of Bac's imagery is evident in the use of water and pergolas as central elements for the arrangement of patios, such as in the Robles León House (1927) or the González Luna House (1929; Figure 1.10). Bac's influence also surfaces in the almost direct morphological loan of selected pieces of his vocabulary, such as the grillwork, wooden grates or the shape of the openings in the house in the new development of Colonias (begun c. 1898) to the west of the old city of Guadalajara.[26] Nevertheless, he gradually moved to a more conscious use of the design devices that were to elevate his work to the standards of an architectural genius: the skilful manipulation of the immaterial, colour, light and shadows, used for the transfiguration of the archetypal spatial boundary of the wall from the role of weight bearer into a meaningful but planar spatial element which bonds with its context, through the distortion of dimensions, varied textures and shapes.

Just like Pikionis, Barragán stands involved during this first period of his work both in the exploration and preservation of popular art and the dissemination of the new ideas reaching Mexico from Europe. Together with fellow students of his, who were to become important architectural figures in Mexico – Ignacio Díaz Morales and Rafael Urzúa Arias – he was part of the 'Group without number or name' that launched the magazine *Bandera de Provincias* (Flag of the Provinces), in 1929.[27] The magazine was in search of a local identity, focusing on provincial culture,[28] and published articles on both local art and international achievement. In its fifth issue, an enthusiastic review of Le Corbusier's *Vers Une Architecture* (1923), which reached Mexico City in 1929, was published. In 1931, Barragán travelled again

FIGURE 1.9 Ferdinand Bac, illustration for the garden behind 'the door with the metallic reflections,' *Les Jardins Enchantés*, 1925.

FIGURE 1.10 Luis Barragán, González Luna House, Guadalajara, 1929.

in Europe, passing en route through New York and becoming acquainted with José Clemente Orozco, a fellow *Tapatío* painter committed to creating 'authentic' Mexican art, and the Viennese architect Friederick Kiesler, who further acquainted him with the work of Adolf Loos and the *raumplan*.[29] The influence of the *raumplan* (different space heights assigned to individual functions) culminated in the second house that Barragán built for himself in Mexico City (1948).

It is after this second trip to Europe, and especially after 1936 when he moved to Mexico City to develop a series of housing projects as a promoter, that Barragán abandoned his quest for identity in order to produce his work that was most close to the International Style, suppressing most evidence of historical references. Nevertheless, like Pikionis, he was not content with the excesses of the modern. This included the transparency of the façade, which he felt could not sustain the privacy and serenity essential in residential spaces, and was not appropriate for the Mexican climate. Like Pikionis, his architecture was too personal for him to comply with the modern ideal of the house as a machine to live in (*machine à habiter*). Thus, it is in the third and last period of his career (after 1940) that he resumed his search for a personal idiom, adapting the rationalist principles of the modern to the Mexican imagery of his youth.

CONCLUSION

Both Barragán and Pikionis are classified under the umbrella term of 'critical regionalism' in Kenneth Frampton's *Modern Architecture: A Critical History*.[30] Together with Gio Ponti, they belong to a long list of architects who were discovered on a global level after the 1960s, when modernity was seriously questioned and its multifarious strands brought forward. They stand out for the uniqueness of their personal idioms, formulated by the reconciliation of the international avant-garde ideals with the typically local, as well as by their ultimate quest for *venustas* (beauty), in times where *utilitas* (functionality) and *firmitas* (firmness) became predominant.[31] For them, beauty is to be traced in the survival of ancient rhythms in the anonymous architecture of local people, constituting the essence of a global, universal truth and connected with a poetic element in design. For Barragán and Pikionis, it is even possible to talk of a universal tradition that enables loans from relevant cultures and places; in this sense, both have been concerned with the Japanese vernacular, the influence of which is apparent in their landscape architecture, in Barragán's gardens in the Pedregal housing development (*see* pages 99–100) and Las Arboledas (Mexico City, 1958), and in Pikionis' Philothei playground (Athens, 1965).

The value of studying their work lies in the fact that they instinctively discern the shortcomings of the modern and test more liberal and expressive interpretations of it, in a time when modernity had become generally accepted. In this sense, their architecture remains timeless and a powerful reference, not least for contemporary iconic, international architectural figures such as Tadao Ando, Peter Zumthor or Steven Holl. This is especially true in terms of craftsmanship, attention to detail, sensorial experience and handling of light, which is inextricably linked with a place's climate and natural resources. The following chapter further focuses on the question of site-specific modern and context, understood in this instance in relation to the aesthetic and symbolic properties of the project's natural surroundings.

CHAPTER 2

MODERNITY AND CONTEXT

Within alternative modernity, national and local identity was often drawn as emphatically from popular lifestyles as from the features of the natural landscape (type and amount of vegetation, land contour and hues of local flora and daylight), with both considered intricately related. This chapter discusses projects that explored the relationship of modernity with its natural surroundings, especially in terms of the building's integration to the land's contour. This particular aspect of the building's conception significantly changed during modernity as a result of advancements in building materials and construction methods. For the mainstream modern, architecture was mostly understood independently from specific places and natural settings; the opposite was true of the alternative modern, where an organic adaptation of the building's form to the land's contour was seen as a conceptual priority. After discussing relevant work of modern masters, we will look at two cases of alternative approaches: the first of an Argentinian architect who demonstrated empathy with the site through his relatively international orientation, and the second of Norwegian modernity, where the site becomes a meaningful parameter of idiomatic architectural expression.

THE SPLIT BETWEEN THE MAN-MADE AND THE NATURAL LANDSCAPE

The first of the 'Five Points of a New Architecture', which Le Corbusier preached in an article published in 1927 in the magazine *L'Esprit Nouveau,* concerned the *pilotis*, the building's support on stilts (piers). Interrelated with the principles of the *plan libre*, the free façade and the ribbon-window, the concept of the *pilotis* was liberating;[1] it allowed for the building's footprint to be minimised, distanced the building from the humidity of the ground and ensured it was properly isolated and aerated. Additionally, the space underneath could conveniently be conceded to circulation and greenery. The building no longer needed to strictly 'respond' to the ground's contour, as its new 'artificial' legs could theoretically land it with relative ease into the most demanding sites.

Pilotis was made possible by the new modular systems of construction. Vertical and horizontal, linear and surface elements, made of reinforced concrete or steel and projected in a grid, allowed for the building's loads to be carried to the ground through isolated supports, instead of continuous, linear masonry. Technological advancements with building materials and methods had already given a boost to construction heights since the end of the previous century, while theoretical works privileged *Hochbau* (high-rise building) over *Flachbau* (low-rise). Walter Gropius' study on the subject, published in 1931, four years after Le Corbusier's Five Points, focused on the higher number of beds and square metres per individual inhabitant that high-rise construction could achieve in comparison with the traditional construction pattern of single-family houses spread on the surface of the ground (the sprawling model).[2]

Nevertheless, high-rise urban planning, as well as the concept of *pilotis*, entailed a certain 'detachment' of the building from its context. They decisively split the man-made from the natural and suggested an alienated relationship of the individual with the ground and its surroundings. People were now contemplating nature and the building's context from a distance, instead of living within it, in harmonious interaction. The same kind of detachment was, for example, inherent in the automobile, within the post-Industrial Revolution world. Although now easier to reach remote destinations, humans had become foreign bodies among nature, marked by and dependent upon the comforts and conformities of the new world that had produced this new means of transport.

THE SPLIT BETWEEN THE 'NEW' AND THE EXISTING

Detachment from the context, at least in conceptual terms, did not merely concern nature but also already existing buildings. The heroic representation of the modern, which was part of its progressive concept, was based on features such as rationality and objectivity, embodied in the geometric abstraction of the avant-garde's volumetric arrangements. The purified aesthetics of avant-garde projects could not be compromised by neighbouring buildings and the eclectic bazaar of the past. Exemplary projects were presented, both by their authors and by architectural critics, in ways that would highlight formal aspects rather than potentially complex relations with their surroundings. In the case of Le Corbusier, this kind of controlled publicity reached the level of a strategic self-promotion through photo-editing, destined to omit details of the context or accentuate selected formal features of the projects.[3]

Erich Mendelsohn's Schocken store in Stuttgart (1926–8) is another example of this type of publicity that missed out on the architect's special effort to adapt to and appropriate the social and urban importance of the site.[4] Often presented in night-time shots, to place emphasis on the transparency and lightness of its façade as well as the dominant, dynamic form of the corner stair tower, the store created an urban landmark for this area of Stuttgart through a direct dialogue with its building context, which was not often represented in relevant publications. The adaptation of the building's entrance to the site's steep contour and the special morphological features, such as the horizontal strips of windows placed in recess among the bands of dark brick of the main façade, follow the characteristics of traditional buildings in this district of the city.

Concerning context in terms of natural surroundings, in *The International Style* of 1932 Henry-Russell Hitchcock and Philip Johnson were designating 'trees and vines' as 'a further decoration for modern architecture', besides architectural details, colours (that should, according to them, be used with restraint) and lettering. They explained, 'Natural surroundings are at once a contrast and a background emphasising the artificial values created by architects'.[5] Context was thus granted merely a supporting role to the powerful images that the modern was expected to create.

Hitchcock and Johnson's three principles of the New Architecture (architecture as volume, instead of mass; regularity of construction and formal expression; and avoidance of applied decoration) were destined to avert 'monstrosities' of the past through a neutral approach that could be applied in different contexts with relatively 'safe' results. This approach was translated in an intention to alter the site as little as possible, by 'landing' the building onto the ground (with the help of its artificial legs), instead of seeking to organically connect its lower part (as well as the rest of its body) with the topography of the site. It culminated in the *tabula rasa* urban planning proposals of the avant-garde, which would feature high-rise housing and neatly arranged homogeneous buildings in the middle of vast, vacant, flat terrains. The negation of architecture's relationship with its context, be it natural or man-made, as a way of universally resolving it proved in the long term to be unrealistic, even dystopic.

FIGURE 2.1 Mies van der Rohe, Farnsworth House, 1945–51.

RETHINKING THE CONTEXT

For reasons both of sanitary construction and of symbolic meaning, another heroic figure of the modern, Mies van der Rohe, 'detached' the building from the ground, elevating it onto an artificial pedestal, a few steps higher than the original ground level. Such an arrangement, reminiscent also of the neoclassical beginnings of his career, is a clear gesture distinguishing the man-made from the natural environment. Mies, who in the 1920s and 1930s delved into a philosophical questioning of human nature and of the role of the modern man in history, believed in the potential of modernity but was never engaged in a social agenda, in the way Walter Gropius, Le Corbusier or Hannes Meyer had, seeking to systematise

MODERNITY AND CONTEXT

construction at an affordable cost. His spaces became increasingly minimal in their functional configuration, but never responded to a concern for minimal dimensions and a standardisation of the housing unit, destined for mass production.

His 1934 project for three patio houses, based on an original design of 1931, was, as the architect Iñaki Ábalos demonstrated, probably destined for single inhabitants.[6] They would be urban, cosmopolitan figures that depended on technical progress to make comfort and refinement possible, while seeking freedom of choice between isolation from and interaction with the busy, urban world surrounding them. With no personal items, except for individual works of art, to evoke specific memories and ties with the past or to hint at the clutter of family life, nature in the patios of these houses is an 'artificial' construct, a man-made landscape that is there for one to contemplate through the extensive transparency of the building envelope. This setting alludes to the cyclical time of nature and life, through the alternation of seasons, as opposed to the linear time of history and progress, which was part of modernity's progressist ideal.

Mies' Farnsworth House (1945–51; Figure 2.1), a post-war masterpiece in Plano, Illinois, is elevated from ground level and accessible through a platform/terrace of concrete arranged on an intermediate level between the house and the ground. The detachment of the construction here is also due to the threat of flooding, because of the house's proximity to a river. In fact, in recent years this proximity has come to be a serious problem for the conservation of the building.[7] The house, a glass box that opens entirely to its surroundings, is situated amid a rich green scenery. It effectively frames views to the outside – given the secluded position of the plot, high walls are not needed for privacy, unlike in his patio houses. Visitors are usually struck by the complete immersion the building allows in nature.

However, nature is there mainly to be viewed, rather than for the user to become part of it by interaction and direct contact. The glazed envelope allows little margin for the appropriation of space by its inhabitant, and provides little indication as to the building's function, geographical context or the tastes of the owner, eventually also inadequately responding to climatic conditions. Although Mies' research regarding the relationship between a completely transparent envelope and its surroundings remains current in works such as Werner Sobek's glass house, R128, in Stuttgart (1999–2000),[8] referring to an urban context, Farnsworth house focuses on the conceptual objectification of the project rather than on anchoring it on the perceptual properties of the site, the lines of the landscape or its texture.

Yet, Mies' projects of the interwar period (plus the earlier Riehl House) featured an intimate relationship with the site, emerging from walls retaining sloping

FIGURE 2.2 Mies van der Rohe, Wolf House, Guben, Poland, 1925–27.

contours in a 'dam-like' way.[9] The Riehl House (Berlin, 1907), otherwise of historicist references, the demolished Wolf House (Guben, Poland, 1925–7; Figure 2.2)[10] and the Tugendhat House (Brno, Czech Republic, 1928–30) are all projects of this type. The Wolf House is considered the first example of the flowing plan in Mies' work, although the construction system is still brick masonry, left apparent. The Tugendhat House is the first whitewashed, purely modern project of his, answering to a personal design process of deconstructing the conventional arrangements of enclosed blocks into three-dimensional planes. These horizontal or vertical elements of no mass interact in space, apparently freely disposed, in the way Theo van Doesburg's counter-compositions work in his canvases.

For Mies, the conversion to the abstract aesthetics of the modern happened relatively late in his professional career. But even for other pioneers of the modern, the response of the building to the site seemed to be the generator of architectural meaning, despite the general view, which was becoming established at the time, that a building should be detached from any notion of site-specific architecture and character corresponding to a particular place. Le Corbusier, having already built Atelier Ozenfant (1922), La Roche House (1923) and Villa Savoye (1928), built a dam-like house in France (the villa for Hélène de Mandrot, Le Pradet, 1929), abandoning the isolated supports of reinforced concrete in favour of load-bearing stone walls. The resulting project was fashioned accordingly to the sloping site and the landscape of the plain to the east of the city of Toulon, extending on one side of the house.[11]

Among the icons of modernity, Frank Lloyd Wright's Fallingwater (Bear Run, Pennsylvania, 1935–7) married the international principles of the New Architecture with a specific site, celebrating an organic relationship between the project and its context, to the point of making it impossible to imagine one without the other. Through its unique approach, this project also confirmed the architect's status as a figure apart from the 'canon', creator of his own lineage of modern tradition.

Aligned with Wright's conceptual intent in Bear Run is a much lesser-known example of modernity in South America, the Casa sobre el Arroyo (House over the Brook; Figure 2.3), in Mar del Plata, Buenos Aires (1943–5). Built by the Argentinian

FIGURE 2.3 Amancio Williams, House over the Brook, Buenos Aires, 1943–45.

architect Amancio Williams (1913–89) for his father, the composer Alberto Williams, the house presents exceptional features in terms of the dialogue it develops with its natural setting, in what was at the time a picturesque spot in the woods, in the suburbs of the Argentinian capital. It is suspended in space, over an elegant arch of reinforced concrete, with foundations looking away from the brook's waterbed and set as far away as possible from it. The brook splits the site in two, while the concrete arch creates a bridge over the water, in the most beautiful part of the setting, reuniting the distinct parts of the site on the house level. Two flights of stairs spread in a mirror arrangement over either section of the arch, materialising the connection in the house's main living space. Combined in plan with a service strip running lengthwise along the house's middle section, the landing, where the staircases meet, essentially divides the house in zones of night-time/service and daytime activities, in a rational, effective manner.

The house can be seen as a powerful gesture, demonstrating the technical potential of its building material, but its sleek form and the straightforward answer it provides to its functional requirements connect it with its context in an unassuming, flowing way. Mirroring the smoothly undulating terrain in which it sits, the house provides a sophisticated answer to the conditions of the site, enhancing the enjoyment one can derive from becoming a part of it. The efficiency of the form must have been due to Williams' background: an aviator, who studied structural engineering before turning to architecture, he creates space within the building's main structural element, while stressing the possibilities of reinforced concrete. The result is a successful negotiation of formal features between the man-made and the natural site.

The same perceptiveness towards the functional demands of the project and also towards the landscape can be detected in an urban scheme by Williams, the first project of his career. In 1942, he designed the Viviendas en el Espacio (Houses in Space; Figure 2.4), a housing development for a site in the southern part of Buenos Aires. This was a series of row houses, arranged on a staggered layout of split levels, so that the roof of one house became a private garden for the next. By exposing the houses' longest sides to the sun and making use of the split levels both for interior and exterior spaces, Williams was able to achieve optimal aeration and lighting conditions for the units and a rationalised access plan for the entire project (a central pathway providing access to the apartments, which also worked as a ventilation device for the units, in conjunction with a stair tower to the south).

Williams' Viviendas were essentially destined for open, flat sites that would allow for the part underneath the housing units to be used for communal, infrastructure, commercial and circulation spaces. Nevertheless, through the arrangement of the green surfaces and the easy slope of the access points, the project had the potential to become a new 'landscape' within the landscape, blending with the natural setting through its private gardens and their overall effect of a green

FIGURE 2.4 Amancio Williams, Houses in Space, project, 1942.

hill. According to this line of thought, Williams' project can be considered as a precursor of projects such as the Siedlung Halen (Halen Estate; Figures 2.5 and 2.6) built by Atelier 5 in Bern, Switzerland, almost two decades later (1956–63).

The Halen Estate became well known internationally as the post-war paradigm of low-rise, high-density housing and an alternative to the hardcore high-rise of modernity which, in the sphere of the intensive post-war reconstruction, began to

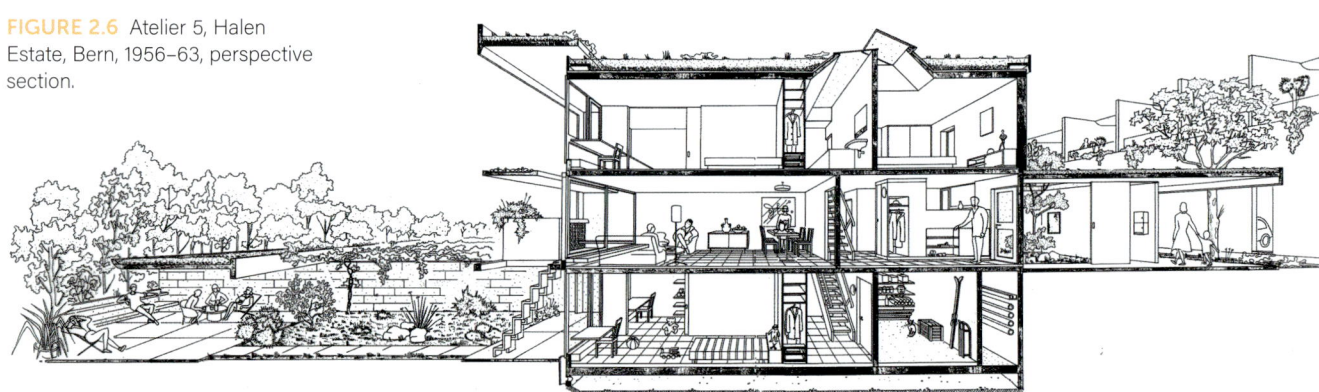

FIGURE 2.5 Atelier 5, Halen Estate, Bern, 1956–63, southern façade.

FIGURE 2.6 Atelier 5, Halen Estate, Bern, 1956–63, perspective section.

show an ugly face of indistinct and excessive use. Evoking ideals of communal life among an enchanting greenery in the southern part of Bern, as well as references of Bern's historical, medieval urban fabric with its long courtyard houses, the Halen Estate remains the embodiment of a modern idea, as a model of mass-production housing in concrete. At the same time, it managed to blend harmoniously with the natural landscape through its adaptation to the site's topography and an effective planning of private and communal spaces of different levels of privacy and greenery, following garden-city ideals of the beginning of the century.

Williams' Viviendas share with Halen Estate the same source of inspiration, Le Corbusier's prototype of mass-production housing, represented in his 1922 Citrohan House and in urban planning projects, such as the Oued Ouchaia proposal for the Durand housing estate in Algeria (1933).[12] Williams changed the individual units' proportions, with respect to Le Corbusier's duplexes of Oued Ouchaia, in order to maximise exposure to the sun and take advantage of the best orientation by assigning the units' longer side to the southern aspect. While in Le Corbusier's project the stepping of the terraced rows corresponds to the double height of the duplex units, Williams used split levels that minimised the overlapping of the rows and secured deep penetration of the winter sun into each apartment. He also made use of the landscaped terrace and its view from the interior, as the main point of contact with the exterior. Because of the split levels, Williams' project could more efficiently address the problem of building on low, sloping sites. His units corresponded to single-bedroom apartments where the increased floor height was covered by a vault of the smooth slope, which created the hill-like terrace in the exterior.

Williams started corresponding with Le Corbusier after World War II, and Le Corbusier offered to publish a piece on Williams' work. In view of this publication and Le Corbusier's invitation for him to be admitted to the next CIAM as a representative of Argentina, Williams travelled in Europe in 1947 and met Le Corbusier in person. Williams, who also collaborated with Emilio Ambasz during the period 1959 to 1962,[13] worked with Le Corbusier on the only project the Franco-Swiss architect built in Argentina: the Curutchet House, in Buenos Aires (1949; Figure 2.7). The house features most of Le Corbusier's devices: *pilotis*, a roof

FIGURE 2.7 Le Corbusier and Amancio Williams, Curutchet House, Buenos Aires, 1949.

terrace, the open plan and an architectural promenade leading from the ground to the upper floor. When Le Corbusier accepted the commission for this house in 1948, he was already working on the project for the new city of Chandigarh in northern India. However, the Curutchet House probably represented for him an opportunity to acquire built work in another country, increasing his fame and impact. Le Corbusier had already visited Argentina in 1929. However, in a letter addressed to Williams, he expressed frustration about the fact that there were no commissions for him there, and that limited discussion existed around his work.

Both Williams' Viviendas and Atelier 5's Halen, with their use of the innovative idea of the green roof, can be considered as heralding the new era of 'green architecture', one of the main avenues the postmodern adopted. In a way, they answer to the same concern for sustainable construction as Frank Lloyd Wright's Jacobs House II, in Middleton, Wisconsin (1948; Figure 2.8). This is a semicircular layout partially imbedded in the ground on its north side, and completely open, through extensive glazing to the south, a precursor of passive solar experiments characteristic of the 1970s.

FIGURE 2.8 Frank Lloyd Wright, Jacobs House II, Middleton, Wisconsin, 1948.

MODERNITY AND CONTEXT

NORWEGIAN MODERATION – A CASE APART

Through their logic of adapting the building to the site's contour and eventually blending the man-made with the natural, all projects mentioned above are close to the ideals guiding modern Norwegian architects of different generations, whose work sets them apart from other Scandinavian architects. Norway has provided a long line of architects who looked to appropriate the basic principles of the modern, such as the rationalisation of the plan, the distinction of functions and the contemporaneity of the working method through adapting it to the specific context of the country, mainly represented in the character and demands of the landscape. Ove Bang (1895–1942) was one of the first to introduce functionalism in Norway. Bang, Knut Knutsen (1903–69) and Arne Korsmo (1900–68) are probably the most influential, first-generation moderns in Norway. As Korsmo's collaborator, Christian Norberg-Schulz, pointed out, Korsmo was more internationally oriented than Bang or Knutsen: 'Whereas Bang always sought the Norwegian, Korsmo looked further afield and saw his work in a wider international context.'[14] However, all three of them inspired the more recent Norwegian modern, and architects such as Sverre Fehn (1924–2009, Pritzker Prize laureate 1997) and Wenche Selmer (1920–98), with their localised approach to modernity.[15]

Bang graduated from the Trondheim Institute of Technology in 1917 and the first years of his career were characterised by buildings that incorporated the persisting neoclassical features of the period. Like Korsmo, Bang travelled within Europe (including Germany and Holland in 1928) and this close acquaintance with the New Architecture greatly influenced him. He moved to Oslo and was soon singled out among his peers for his designs for a traditional housing type – cabins that successfully combined modern features of an abstract geometrical approach, both in plan and in elevation, with the Norwegian landscape. His functionalist project of the Villa Stousland II, in Sogn, Oslo (1935; Figure 2.9), features a flat roof and a large glazed surface facing south, incorporating direct access from the villa's living space to the garden and expressing the close relationship of the Norwegian people with nature and country life. The villa's prismatic forms and clean lines, with the introduced flat roof and its wooden walls painted white, clearly recall Le Corbusier's 1926 Paris Pavilion. During 1935–6, Bang collaborated with the Czech architect Jan Reiner (1909–2010), who had earlier worked in Paris with Le Corbusier.

Still, Villa Stousland focuses on a close connection with its green surroundings and the landscape of woods, blending well with it through the rhythm of the wooden boards of its envelope, remaining apparent under their white finish. Most importantly, through the treatment of the house's threshold as a separate transition

FIGURE 2.9 Ove Bang, Villa Stousland II, Sogn, Oslo, 1935.

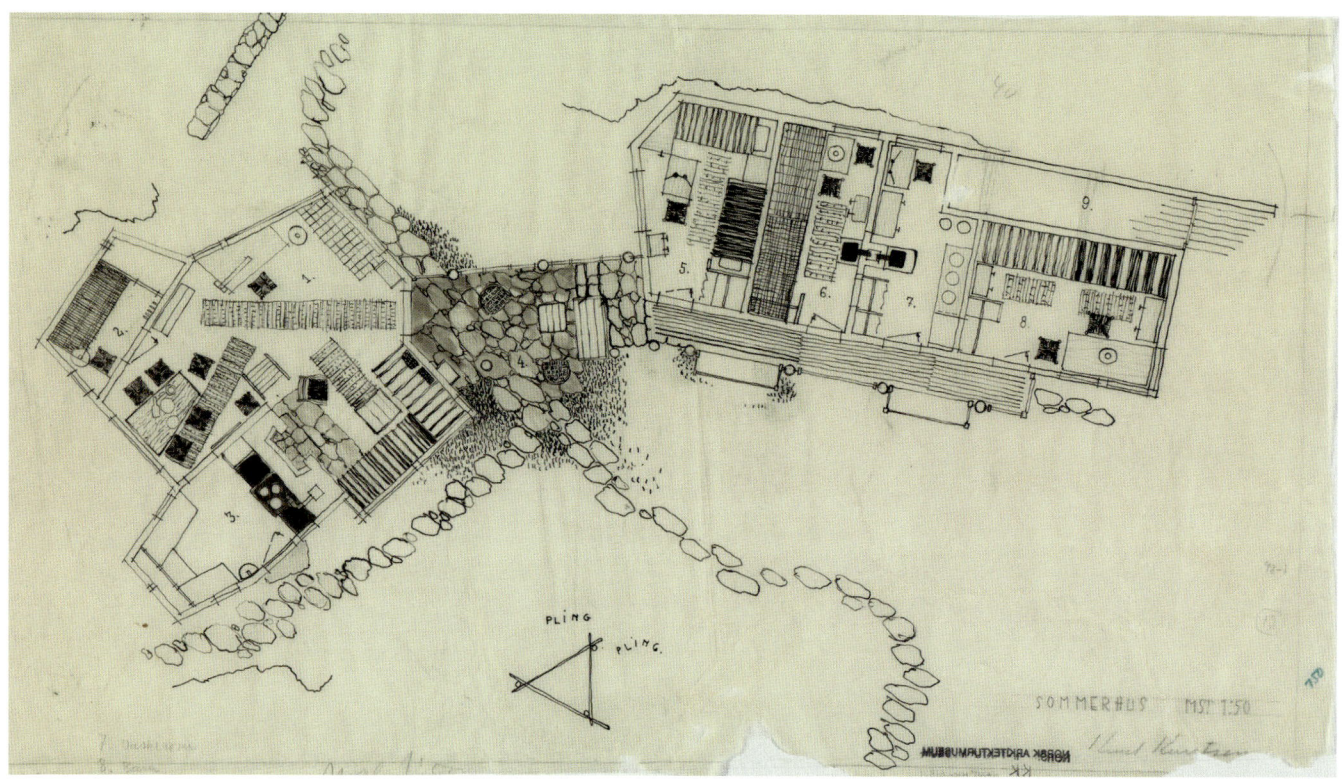

FIGURE 2.10 Knut Knutsen, summer cottage, Portø, northeasatern Norway, 1949, plan.

space, the project directly evokes the local, rural lifestyle. This is a feature that also distinguishes Wenche Selmer's work.

Knut Knutsen's summer cottage in Portø, northeastern Norway, (1949; Figures 2.10 and 2.11) adapts to its context through the use of wood as the construction material, but also through the oblique and asymmetrical form of the building, which seems to directly emerge from the landscape. As Norberg-Schulz reports, rationing was still in place during these years after World War II, so the architect had to build the house from waste wood, thus underlining its informal character. The house is divided in two parts, the main living space and the night-time zone being linked together by a terrace, protected by the same continuous, irregular roof. Open-air access to the individual rooms underpins the house's openness to nature and

FIGURE 2.11 Knut Knutsen, summer cottage, Portø, northeasatern Norway, 1949, exterior view.

FIGURE 2.12 Wenche Selmer, architect's house, Gråkammen, Oslo, 1963.

FIGURE 2.13 (*opposite*) Wenche Selmer, summerhouse, Hellersøya, south coast of Norway, 1965, detail from the house's exterior spaces and the wooden docks.

its skewed forms mirror the lines of the rocky woods surrounding it. Knutsen's approach to construction is an obvious reference to the work of Sverre Fehn, such as Fehn's Nordic Pavilion in Venice (1962), literally a building planned around the trees found on site, celebrating its topography and famously reproducing the conditions of a Nordic, subdued light.

Perhaps establishing a more direct connection with Knutsen's architectural ideals about 'being in harmony with nature' and 'subordinating houses to it' is Wenche Selmer (1920–98), who has acknowledged Knutsen as the greatest influence on her work.[16] The house that Selmer designed together with her husband, Jens Andreas Selmer (in Oslo, 1963; Figure 2.12), was awarded the Sundt Prize (1964–5) for outstanding architecture and is representative of her sensitive approach to the landscape, with wood being her primary material of choice. The house is one of the best instances of her work, the majority of which consists of summerhouses (Figure 2.13) or detached suburban houses with a low-key profile, minimal budgets and exquisite attention to construction details. Balancing private and professional life, Selmer produced mostly small-scale buildings which feature efficient functional arrangements and a refined approach to everyday living, in all its

simplicity. Drawing inspiration from traditional summerhouses surrounded by rocky hills and woods along the Norwegian coastline, her buildings sit in the site with minimal encroachment, often on the most appropriate spot within a limited terrain, in order both to protect the dwelling from the climatic conditions and to endow it with a choice of views and relative space comfort in terms of everyday needs.

The architect and theoretician Elisabeth Tostrup explains how Selmer carefully placed the house's openings (doors and windows) in such a way as to achieve optimal proportions for the interior spaces, which manage to appear more spacious than they actually are. This is, of course, a modern idea in its essence. Tostrup classifies Selmer with the group of Norwegian architects that 'practised the difficult art of making tradition contemporary, of innovation and selection in the treasure house of history without being trapped by sentimentalism'.[17] She highlights one specific feature of Selmer's architecture that seems to be common in the work of architects demonstrating an empathy for the site: the respect for the setting embodied in the transition between the building and the terrain, in this case the rocky grounds of the Norwegian coast or the wet and cold ground of the forest inland. She also describes her architecture as 'a stand against the hegemony of consumerism', and it is certainly an example to follow in the present materialistic era.[18] Selmer chose to follow the contour of the terrain as far as possible, where these conceptual and physical 'borderlines' between the man-made and the natural setting are concerned. It is on these points that the kinship of her architecture both with the traditional constructions and the modern advancements can be read.

The lineage of Norwegian modernity discussed here takes up perceptual properties of the site, as picked up in the lines of the contour, and strives to transpose them into architecture. Although the building outcome may vary a lot in terms of its formal expression, these projects are based on the principle of modelling architecture in conjunction with the landscape, which was also manifested in Amancio Williams' work. Williams remained fascinated by concrete and by modernity's collective living agenda, whereas the Norwegians sought a closer link with the place through lifestyle and materials, and deliberately low-key interventions. Thus, there is no question of the man-made competing with the natural context in object-like buildings; architecture is established as an inseparable part and a continuation of its setting. This connection will be further explored in the following chapter, by discussing the use of materials and colours that blend modernity not only with its natural but also with its social landscape.

CHAPTER 3

MATERIALS AND COLOURS

For a wide public, modernity has been marked either by the monochromatic choices and whitewashed walls of the avant-garde, or by the monotony of grey established in a large part of our built environment through the broad use of bare reinforced concrete. The fact that an even rougher version of concrete dominated the work of modernity's Third Generation has rather enhanced this perception. Yet this has not been the case with many lineages of the modern and especially with alternative facets of it, where colour and building materials became the embodiment of an architectural imagery closely linked with local culture.

This chapter addresses the use of colour in modernity and its alternative expressions, as well as the way in which colour is intrinsically connected with the use of specific materials. It is, indeed, astonishing how few critical essays discuss the effect materials have on the chromatic configuration of an architectural project or the ways in which colour can be inherently connected with the use of a specific material and how it uniquely characterises an architectural work. Materials and colours are closely connected, based on their power to modify architectural space through their visual effects. Using Luis Barragán, an architect most renowned for his research in relation to colour, as a starting point, this chapter tackles the way colour was understood in three-dimensional space by dominant approaches of the modern. It concludes with examples of architects whose work is characterised by the use of specific materials, and the colour palette these materials offer.

THE BARRAGÁN COLOUR UNIVERSE

Perhaps the most celebrated work of Luis Barragán is his own house and studio, the second that he built for himself in Francisco Ramírez Street, Tacubaya, Mexico City (1947). Together with the Gilardi House (1976), which also originates from the last and longest period of his architectural production, these two houses are considered the apotheosis of Barragán's industrious manipulation of light into space and of his dextrous handling of the multicoloured surfaces of walls.

Barragán's palette is a mixture of traditional Mexican hues, the ones surviving in him through childhood memories or inspired by the work of artist friends, such as Chucho Reyes,[1] as well as of colour schemes connected with European masters, such as the Bauhaus teachers Josef Albers and Johannes Itten.[2] Although a devout

Catholic, after moving to Mexico City at the beginning of the 1940s, Barragán moved in artistic circles of a communist inclination, notably the one around Diego Rivera and his wife Frida Kahlo. He frequently visited, as did Chucho Reyes and many other Mexican artists of the period, Frida Kahlo's traditional Casa Azul (Blue House; Figure 3.1) in Coyoácan, Mexico City.³

Rivera and Kahlo were at the time figureheads of the country's artistic developments and their interest in Mexico's colourful past could not be diverted, not even in the purely functionalist house that the architect Juan O'Gorman built for them in San Ángel, one of Mexico City's well-off residential areas, in 1931–2

FIGURE 3.1 Casa Azul, Frida Kahlo's family house, Coyoácan, Mexico City, c. 1904.

MATERIALS AND COLOURS

(Figure 3.2).[4] O'Gorman, who was then a great fan of Le Corbusier's, used many of the ideas Le Corbusier materialised in his Amedée Ozenfant House and Studio (1923), including an outdoor spiral staircase and floor-to-ceiling windows in the studio.[5] The Rivera Kahlo House comprises two separate cubic buildings connected by a narrow bridge at the level of the flat roof, close to Rivera's bedroom. O'Gorman used a cactus fence to border the plot from the side of the main street, as well as the characteristic indigo blue of Kahlo's traditional house in Coyoácan and a terracotta colour to differentiate the two sections of the house. As Valerie Fraser points out, 'The use of colour in the Rivera-Kahlo house is especially interesting in that it could be interpreted as both Mexican and modern.'[6] Similarly strong colours can be found in Le Corbusier's Esprit Nouveau pavilion or his Pessac housing (both dating from 1926). This parallel, according to Fraser, is possibly generated by common Mediterranean roots and tastes.

The same indigo hue was used by Barragán in some of his early residential work in his hometown of Guadalajara. In the more 'intentional and consistent use of colour'[7] that Juan Palomar sees in Cristo House (Guadalajara, 1929) and the bold hues that Barragán applies in the framing and latticework of the house's openings, one can recognise elements of his mature work, such as his studio house in Tacubaya (1947; Figure 3.3) and the Gilardi House.

Colour is one essential component of Barragán's architecture. It is closely connected with the use of specific materials and textures, often mixed with the thick plaster and roughcast that the architect regularly used. His vibrant hues and diversified textures aim at staging unique spatial experiences. The most striking choices regarding the colour scheme of Barragán's house and studio are created in conjunction with Mathias Goeritz's outspoken art and with the use of varied materials for architectural elements with a sculptural quality in space.[8] The golden hue of Goeritz's painting, hung in the middle landing of the main staircase and naturally lit from above, becomes a source of light for the house's entrance hall, through its reflective quality. The mellow dark ochre of the freestanding, wooden steps leading from the open space of the living-room/library up to a mezzanine replaces the lava stone flooring of the main staircase. This unexpected use of a traditional material adds a warm touch in the otherwise austere ambiance of the

FIGURE 3.2 Juan O'Gorman, Rivera Kahlo House, San Ángel, Mexico City, 1931–32.

FIGURE 3.3 Luis Barragán's house and studio, Tacubaya, Mexico City, 1947, main living space and staircase to the mezzanine.

place. Additionally, the steps create a continuum with the mid-height door of the mezzanine, which unfolds vertically in space and cuts through the white roughcast of the adjacent walls. The horizontally running grain of the wood, accentuated by the direction of the door's boards, contrasts the room's verticality, as expressed in the double height of the living room/library.

Above all, the importance of Barragán's chromatic compositions lies in the way space is modelled with colour, transformed and perceived through it. As the architect pointed out, 'Colour is a complement to the architecture. It serves to enlarge or reduce a space. It's also useful for adding that touch of magic a place needs.'[9] It is part of the poetry that Barragán sought to create with and within space. He decided on colours once the building was already in place but was in no way finished.[10] He took time to select the colour scheme with the help of mock-ups and endeavoured to experience the built space to the full before handing it over to its end users.[11]

When speaking of the main sources of inspiration for his architecture, Barragán did so in terms of colours and light, evoking memories from traditional architecture: 'The unassuming architecture of the village and provincial towns of my country have been a permanent source of inspiration. Such, for instance, the whitewashed walls; the peace to be found in patios and orchards; the colorful streets; the humble majesty of the village squares surrounded by shady open corridors.'[12]

Gilardi House stands out for the stark yellow colour of the glass used for the indoor, slit-windows that mark the house's entrance. Equally, the magenta wall of the patio, coloured after the flowers of the existing Jacaranda tree, dominates the view from the living room and enlivens its ambiance. A non-load-bearing wall, it becomes an architectural device which effectively organises the house around it, thus materialising its core, albeit independently from its structural system.

At the same time, Barragán's use of colour is based on schemes studied by the Bauhaus masters Josef Albers and Johannes Itten, in their respective works *Interaction of Colour* and *The Art of Colour*, which were both included in Barragán's extensive library.[13] This is true for the patio wall, as well as for the two adjacent walls around the interior pool of the Gilardi House, which are painted in the same hue of cobalt blue, and 'depending on one's angle of view, ... either form a box of light or wipe out the corner of the room'.[14] These examples refer both to the interaction of pure colours, such as the ones typical in Barragán's palette (pink, yellow, blue, purple) and to the spatial relationships that can be created by juxtaposing warm and cold hues (volumes that advance or retreat depending on the colour applied).

Another feature of Barragán's colour schemes is the fact that colour is frequently applied on all sides of the wall, including the edge. This approach transforms the partition walls in his spaces, especially when these are freestanding, into interacting, planar, spatial elements, and distinguishes Barragán's compositions from those of De Stijl masters, where edges are often painted in complementary colours to differentiate opposing structural directions. Barragán's use of colour essentially matches the approach of Le Corbusier, who created, accentuated and classified space through colour. Mathias Goeritz also underlined this connection by pointing out the distinctive ability of both Barragán and Le Corbusier to place emphasis in the architecture's spiritual values.[15]

It is interesting, at this point, to look more closely at the differences and parallels between the approaches, regarding colour, of Le Corbusier and De Stijl, as these are most commonly mentioned in relation to the mainstream modern.

VOLUMES AND PLANES – CONFIGURING COLOUR AND FORM

Le Corbusier began systematically using colour after World War II, notably during the last period of his career. Maisons Jaoul (Neuilly-sur-Seine, 1951), with their twin brick domes and earthy colours, have been particularly significant for Le Corbusier's 'turn' towards local methods of construction, integration to the site and appreciation of local craftsmanship.[16] However, colour had preoccupied Le Corbusier, not only from a practical but also from a theoretical point of view, since a much earlier point in his career; surprisingly enough, in a period that his architectural genius was mediatised through the whitewashed exterior walls of the Villa Savoye (Poissy, 1928) or the Villa Stein-de-Monzie ('Les Terrasses', Garches, Vaucresson, 1926). Few are familiar with the work that Le Corbusier undertook on colour compositions during the interwar period, starting with his essay on architectural polychromy and the first chromatic palette created for the wallpaper brand Salubra in 1931.[17] In his ground-breaking work on the subject, Arthur Rüegg called into question even Le Corbusier's purist 'white' period, by re-examining the colours intended by the architect for the Villa Savoye and underscoring the concept of an architectural space whose poetic qualities, enhanced by the use of colour, are inherently linked with its psychological effects.[18]

Le Corbusier's approach is essentially different from the 'floating planes' that the De Stijl masters, such as Piet Mondrian and Theo van Doesburg, proposed. For them, vertical and horizontal planes in space are rarely associated with the building's functional or tectonic qualities, a fact probably associated with a decisive breach in modernity's critical discourse between colours and the building's construction process and materials. The De Stijl approach to colour is marked by the artistic concept of a 'universal harmony', which is based on the use of a restricted palette limited to the primary colours red, yellow and blue and the non-colours white, grey and black, the deconstruction technique and right angles. These compositions are characteristically celebrated in the abstract, purely geometrical canvases of Mondrian or in Van Doesburg's elementarist counter-compositions.

Le Corbusier was also influenced by Van Doesburg, especially after the work of the latter was exhibited in the 1923 *Galerie L'Effort Moderne* exhibition in Paris.[19] References to Van Doesburg's counter-construction project can be found in the hallway of the Maisons La Roche-Jeanneret, Paris (the design of which began in 1922–3), especially in the way the walls are stacked up as planes and painted in white with light-blue edges.[20] However, Le Corbusier was essentially interested in 'eminently architectural colours'[21] and their 'constructive qualities'.[22] Additionally, he associated colour with moods and their psychological effects: colour 'modifies space', 'classifies objects', and finally 'acts physiologically upon us and reacts strongly upon our sensitivities'.[23]

To achieve his goal to 'create tension and ambiance' in space through colour's physical and psychological effects, Le Corbusier limited his palette to the use of yellow-ochre, red, brown, white, black, ultramarine and their mixed tones, all colours to be found also in the classical tradition.²⁴ In his 1931 *Salubra* collection, Le Corbusier introduced 43 monochromatic tones, in mostly pastel shades, made up in their majority from natural colour pigments (therefore easy to reproduce in most circumstances) deriving from 12 basic colours, ultramarine, ochre and earth colours. He aimed at combinations of three to five colours achieved using pattern cards describing colour moods (Figure 3.4).

Le Corbusier used colour to camouflage and fine-tune the space's proportions (although never to intentionally fake the actual spatial dimensions), by either dissolving or underpinning certain volumes through their uniform treatment in specific colours.²⁵ Thus, he essentially 'built' volumes, while De Stijl was mainly interested in 'unfolding' them. For the artists of De Stijl, space is visually 'exploded' into an 'open sculpture', through the complementary use of colour and form: vertical and horizontal planes are differentiated in colour.²⁶ As a result, De Stijl has often been viewed as an architectural current that placed interest primarily in architecture's aesthetic outcome. The few built projects considered as

FIGURE 3.4 Le Corbusier, Colour Keyboard, *Atmosphère*, 1931.

RETHINKING MODERNITY

representative of it, notably Café de Unie in Rotterdam by Jacobus Johannes Pieter Oud (1925) and Schröder House, built in Utrecht by Gerrit Rietveld (1924), are not usually discussed in relation to tectonic properties.

Schröder House became an icon of modernity for its colour and functional configuration. By 'discontinuing' corners and edges, Rietveld created the impression of a 'house of cards', made of fragmented spatial snapshots, as opposed to the space *continuos* that Le Corbusier sought to establish along his architectural promenades (on this issue, see also the analysis in Chapter 5). At the same time, this approach allowed for a functional organisation of great flexibility and alternative configurations, depending on the Schröder family's habits and varied needs in time.

De Stijl has influenced Scandinavian architects, such as the Norwegian Arne Korsmo (*see* page 56), who is distinguished among the representatives of Norwegian modernity for his use of colour and for the flexibility of the layout manifested in mature works of his, such as his own house in Planetveien 12 in Oslo (1952–5).[27] Korsmo also worked on several interior design commissions (interior arrangement of stores and exhibition spaces). Still, his interwar production features robust volumetric compositions, enhanced by the use of colours in their distinct parts, and firmly rooted in the grounds through split levels; sequences of transition spaces protected by pergolas, such as the ones used in his Villa Dammann in Oslo (1930), belie the rigidity of the pure building geometry.

Korsmo had visited Holland with a travel grant obtained after his studies and had been impressed with the work of the Dutch masters, especially Marinus Dudok (with whom Oud had worked initially and whose most well-known project, the town hall of Hilversum, was still under construction in 1931).[28] This influence can be detected in the absence of hierarchy characterising the grid of the main façade of his Villa Stenersen (1937; Figure 3.5) in Oslo and the use of the complementary blue and orange shades in the two upper floors.[29] The overall configuration of the house's façades in glass, steel and polished white concrete, as well as the house's free plan, also show influences from Le Corbusier.

MATERIALS AND COLOURS

FIGURE 3.5 Arne Korsmo, Villa Stenersen, Oslo, 1937.

Korsmo's work is characterised by his functionalist, mainly internationally orientated approach, but also by a purely personal style and extreme attention to detail.[30] His colour scheme for the Villa Dammann marries his 'Korsmo blue' shade with the expressive, semicircular form of the study, while the fragmentation of volumes and the use of colours in the interior still recall De Stijl compositions. The colour scheme of the house in Planetveien, a project built in collaboration with his student and biographer Christian Norberg-Schulz, was devised together with his wife, Grete, who was an enamel artist, and their painter friend Gunnar S. Gundersen.[31] In the functional polyphony of the scheme, the influence of Charles and Ray Eames, who had become close friends of Arne and Grete Korsmo, must have been equally decisive.[32]

MATERIALS AND THEIR DISTINCTIVE COLOURS

As already mentioned, differences between modernity's various mainstream approaches may have contributed to conventional critical discourses that discussed materials mostly in relation to tectonics (the ability of an architectural work to stand), while seeing colours as an isolated part of the architectural work.[33] On the other hand, such an attitude must also have been due to the fact that photography, especially of the sort used in specialised publications, has had only a relatively recent life in colour. The broad use of colour photographs in the press dates mainly from the middle of the 20th century. There existed before that a relatively limited capability for visualising colour.[34] Black-and-white representations of architecture brought forward primarily formal and volumetric properties of buildings; this was true even for work marked by the choice of building materials, such as the architecture of Frank Lloyd Wright or Alvar Aalto.

Peter Blundell Jones offers the example of the students of the Architectural Association in London visiting Mies van der Rohe's Barcelona Pavilion (1929). They had known the project for decades as a mythical building, detached from its context, in black-and-white photographic shots which, although allowing viewers to distinguish between different construction materials, provided no information about their specific hues and shades. 'The biggest shock ... was the colour, not transmissible in the black and white photographic versions we had known, and felt as a newly bestowed gift.'[35]

Aris Konstantinidis (1913–93) is one architect whose work is characterised by a unique structural and functional approach, combined with a very personal style in the use of construction materials, which can only be appreciated with real-life visits. Although a generation younger than Dimitris Pikionis (*see* pages 7–13), Konstantinidis is often discussed in parallel with his mentor for three main reasons: his own interest in the tradition of the place, especially through popular, local craftsmanship; his polemical approach to architecture and design, which is easily juxtaposed to Pikionis' temperamental, yet relatively low-profile, Socratic strategy to both practising and teaching; and the undeniable impact they both had on generations of architects in Greece.[36] The ingenuity of his work is difficult to perceive without physically visiting the place and admiring the distinct hue

MATERIALS AND COLOURS

of the local stone, as integrated in his site-specific structures. His construction system emphasised the grid, distinguishing vertical and horizontal elements: the standard reinforced concrete frame, complete with masonry infill for the walls, was replaced by load-bearing stone masonry and reinforced concrete slabs and beams. One of Konstantinidis' innovations was the frequent use of 'inverse' beams that supported the roof while protruding from the upper side of the slab, allowing for the load-bearing elements and the glazed parts of the façade to rise without interruption from floor to ceiling.

In a way, Konstantinidis' rational, functionalist compositions are close to the construction system tested by Le Corbusier in the villa for Madame Hélène de Mandrot,[37] in Le Pradet, France (1929; *see* page 28), or in his Errazuris House project for a coastal site in Chile (1930).[38] Villa Mandrot began as a standardised steel housing project and ended up as a stone construction embedded in its mountainous setting.[39] Presenting the villa in his *Œuvre Complète*, Le Corbusier stated that despite the use of stone masonry for the walls, his usual conceptual principle for a clear classification between primary vertical and secondary, horizontal construction elements, as well as glazed walls, applied in this house.[40]

In Konstantinidis' case, wood is frequently used for the openings' frames and casements; openings often cover entire steps of the grid. Yet the architect takes care to adapt the extensive glazed surfaces to the climate and needs of the place. The grid extends to spaces of transition between the inside and the outside, almost always protected by extensions of the flat roof. These are meant to temper weather conditions and help the building 'react' in accordance with their ever-changing nature. Konstantinidis' whitewashed concrete elements counterbalance the chromatic kinship between locally sourced stone used for the walls and the rocky landscape. At the same time, they introduce, as the theorist David Leatherbarrow points out, a 'sense of care' applied by the humans to the building in an effort to resist the adverse natural elements and their corrosive effects, as well as to renew the construction across various stretches of time.[41] This kind of 'concordant' existence of architecture can only be understood by real-life visits to the site, during which one can appreciate the light lemon ochre that connects the land with the walls that were born from it, in the flooding daylight. A representative

FIGURE 3.6 Aris Konstantinidis, weekend house, Aegina island, 1975, exterior view.

FIGURE 3.7 Aris Konstantinidis, weekend house, Aegina island, 1975, portico.

example are certain houses that Konstantinidis built on the island of Aegina – the residence and studio of the prominent Greek painter Nikos Moralis (1974–8) and a small weekend house (1975; Figures 3.6 and 3.7). Konstantinidis' personal style has been developing with regards to the building's adaptation to the site from his first important commission, the Eftaxias weekend house in Eleusis, Attica (1938–40), and its white-plastered volumes, to Kakrides House in Sykia (1951) and its stone-bearing walls and reinforced concrete horizontal structural zones.[42]

It would be pertinent to note here that in Greece, the new material,[43] concrete cast on site, met with huge success, due to its relative compatibility with the country's climate, and the natural and human resources it required.[44] In the course of years, its treatment and finish – in terms both of the natural pigments that its components contain, resulting in specific, site-relating colours, and of various

MATERIALS AND COLOURS

FIGURE 3.8 George Makris and Yota Kalavritinou, holiday house, Aegina island, 1993–98.

techniques to achieve a unique palette of textures that are often transplanted in the research with other materials, like brick and pre-fabricated concrete blocks – acquired a special importance, one often uniquely marking the work of certain architects. This has been the case with Kyriakos Krokos,[45] George Makris (Figure 3.8)[46] or Michalis Souvatzidis.[47] In the Vettas residence (Figure 3.9), built in Filothei, Athens (1989–91) just a few years before his untimely death, Krokos was reportedly seeking to replicate the colour of the Attica sunset in the customised bricks used for the buildings.[48] This work represents a perfect chromatic marriage between the earthy and muted tones of distinct materials: the yellow ochre of the stone, the brown ochre of the brick, the sepia of the floor marbles, the warm yellowish grey of the mosaic of etched concrete, all achieved with the help of natural pigments,

FIGURE 3.9 Kyriakos Krokos, Vettas residence, Filothei, Athens, 1989–91.

MATERIALS AND COLOURS

contrasting with the turquoise of the industrially produced metal windows and other secondary parts. The project brings forward many morphological elements that are typical of Krokos' work and of his localised version of the modern, such as the crowning patterns of the concrete columns, the semicircular balcony and the perforated metal or brick parapets.

The golden or silver reflective hues that Souvatzidis applies onto oblique interior surfaces that frame skylight openings in his buildings (Figure 3.10) are reminiscent of Art Nouveau and even Art Deco techniques, such as Henry van de Velde's doors at the Hôtel Wolfers, Brussels (as early as 1929),[49] or Arne Korsmo's ceiling at the entrance of the Villa Dammann. They also recall the use of Mathias Goeritz's golden hues in Barragán's House; in this instance, they take on an additional role of reflecting the heat of the Mediterranean climate in an environmentally friendly architecture, oscillating between the vernacular and the advanced technology by the adoption of passive energy devices. Souvatzidis' architectural production is primarily marked by the use of concrete blocks as a structural material; he manages to create various chromatic shades with specially selected aggregates and natural pigments, thus enhancing the specificity of his work.

To conclude, the topicality of the work of architects such as Barragán, who have become iconic figures of the modern through their unique, individual interpretations of colour, can be seen in subsequent works, either in the same geographical context, such as Ricardo Legorreta's colourful buildings, or in different ones, as in the bright yellow and magenta pre-cast, ribbed concrete walls of Les Graines D'Étoiles nursery (Figures 3.11 and 3.12) by Atelier Fernandez, in Aix-en-Provence, France, 2009.[50]

Legorreta's Camino Real Hotel (Figure 3.13), built shortly before the Summer Olympics of 1968 in Mexico City, as well as the Graines D'Étoiles project, revisit Barragán's language not only from the point of view of their bright colours, but most importantly in the organisation of the plan. In the former project, colours serve as cultural ambassador (originally the colours used by Legorreta were red, pink, yellow, orange, brown and gold), while in the latter they serve as designator of

FIGURE 3.10 Michalis Souvatzidis, Arts Centre Building, Athens, 1992–7.

MATERIALS AND COLOURS

FIGURE 3.11 Atelier Stéphane Fernandez, Les Graines D'Étoiles nursery, Aix-en-Provence, 2009, exterior.

FIGURE 3.12 Atelier Stéphane Fernandez, Les Graines D'Étoiles nursery, Aix-en-Provence, 2009, interior.

FIGURE 3.13 Ricardo Legorreta, Camino Real Hotel, Mexico City, 1968.

social function. As for the configuration of their layouts, both projects are organised around interior courtyards that promote privacy. Despite their different functions and sizes, both buildings are introverted; their envelopes give little away about their interiors, just as Barragán's houses usually turned their back on the street. The following chapter deals with an opposite conceptual strategy, where familiar imagery becomes a statement of kinship imprinted on the building's skin.

CHAPTER 4

THE FORBIDDEN WOR(L)D: ORNAMENT AND DECORATION IN THE ALTERNATIVE MODERN

In 1908 Adolf Loos published his text *Ornament and Crime*, which has since set the standards for modern architecture and its detachment (at least on a theoretical basis) from 'ornamentation'. In the text, Loos announced, 'The evolution of culture is synonymous with the removal of ornament from objects of daily use,' and named any tendency of a civilised person to continue producing ornate objects as 'degenerate'.[1] He declared, 'Ornament is wasted manpower and therefore wasted health. ... But today it also means wasted material, and both mean wasted capital.'[2] Loos' ideas were echoed by Le Corbusier in his book *Decorative Art of Today* (1925), a collection of articles already published in *L'Esprit Nouveau* which was actually all about a decorative art that 'is not decorated'.[3]

In an effort to define modern architecture and its role in the cultural development of a modern society, the criminalisation of ornament was sped along both by Loos' aphorisms and the impact of Henry-Russell Hitchcock and Philip Johnson's Third Principle of *The International Style* (1932), which preached the avoidance of applied decoration. Almost 25 years after the first appearance of Loos' text, on the other side of the Atlantic, Hitchcock and Johnson picked up the subject, this time in a style-defining discourse, which in many cases praised the unaffected way in which European functionalists dealt with the modern structural methods against the approach of their American counterparts.[4] In their opinion, Europeans clearly differentiated 'skeleton construction' from its enveloping 'protective screen', and therefore explicitly emphasised the effect of volume, or of the 'open box' that the architecture of reinforced concrete or of metallic parts in grille dictated. Americans, on the other hand, still frequently went out of their way to produce an effect of mass, linked with traditional construction methods of load-bearing walls.

Loos passed away in 1933, a year after the publication of Hitchcock and Johnson's *The International Style*; by then his text had already been elevated to the status of a functionalist 'manual'. Loos rejected ornament in utilitarian, everyday objects based on a self-evident cultural advancement that made it superfluous and redundant for the aesthetic pleasure of the cultivated and refined modern person. In other words, the modern person had progressed so much that he or she had in fact 'outgrown ornament', and no longer needed it as a source of aesthetic pleasure in life.[5] Like Loos, Hitchcock and Johnson also took the absence of ornamentation as an effective means 'to differentiate [at least, *editor's note*] superficially the current style from the styles of the past and from the various manners of the last century and a half.'[6]

When it was published in 1932, the cover of *The International Style* featured a pencil-drawn image of Le Corbusier's Villa Savoye, 'evidently traced straight off a photograph.'[7] Discussing the power of photographic representations regarding the modern and our perception of it in terms of its avant-garde architecture and masters, Blundell Jones comments, 'Villa Savoye is the epitome of abstract architecture, shorn of texture and materiality, and of the clutter of eaves and ridges, mouldings and cornices, that had defined visually the essence of traditional building.'[8] For what else could the prescribed absence of decoration refer to primarily if not to the heterogeneous assortment of a 19th-century eclectic building's façade? However, in this respect, Loos' axioms become unclear when one considers the effect of the polished marble on the ground floor façade and the shop's interiors in his celebrated Goldmann and Salatch building (Vienna, 1909–11). Despite the geometric simplicity and the classical proportions of the general composition that created sensation when the building was inaugurated at the beginning of the century, one has difficulty explaining how the luxurious, patterned material Loos used to clad parts of the building is not what would traditionally be considered as adornment.

The absence of ornamentation equally called for sober interiors and unpretentious ambiances, again terms which could not accurately describe Loos' interiors, usually completed by especially designed, built-in pieces of furniture. His wife's bedroom in their Vienna apartment (1903; Figure 4.1) was entirely covered by fur and cloth: blue carpet on the floor, overlain with white angora fleece and *batiste rayée* on the walls to provide a room of pleasure and relaxation and a perfect, appropriate fit for the function it sought to fulfil.[9] His architecture has been described as 'the envelope of a body.'[10] Nevertheless, both the bedroom and the luxurious materials of his clothing stores are instances of self-indulgence, an allusion to a sensual, sybaritic way of life that opposes the austerity of means advocated for by the architect.[11] On this point, José Lahuerta argues that *Ornament and Crime* was not addressing architecture at all. According to him, when the text finds its place in the timeline of Loos' theoretical and design work, as well as of contemporary theoreticians from which

FIGURE 4.1 Interior of Adolf Loos' apartment, Vienna, 1903; his wife's bedroom.

he was deeply influenced, it becomes plain that he intended to tackle the subject of ornamentation merely in the context of everyday objects, which due to excessive and pointless decoration had indeed become alienated from their principal functional roles.[12] This argument is persuasive, additionally explaining why it was so difficult to completely strip architecture from all kinds of decoration, especially when it concerned relatively well-off lifestyles.

Hitchcock and Johnson's *The International Style* stood apart from the manifesto-like tone and pseudoscientific discourse of Loos' *Ornament and Crime*. Hitchcock and Johnson distanced themselves from axiomatic prescriptions for producing architecture and even added, 'It would be ridiculous to state categorically that there will never be successful applied ornament in architecture again.'[13] The remark proved prophetic: in the space of one decade, mainstream trends would change drastically, even with respect to the work of the by then established avant-garde. The revival of ornamentation marked the alternative approaches to the modern of countries like Mexico and Brazil.

In these contexts, architects had focused on a synergy between art and architecture since the interwar period and considered ornamentation an inherent part of their countries' complex cultural existences and identities. Murals became the most important manifestation of such tendencies in the work of many Mexican and Brazilian modern architects. In Europe perhaps the most representative case is that of the Italian modern, especially of the Milan school, whose work was highlighted after World War II by the editorial efforts of Ernesto Nathan Rogers in the magazines *Domus* and *Casabella-Continuità*. The course of this aesthetic shift can be followed through the work of prominent architectural figures in these geographical backgrounds.

MURALISM AND MEXICAN MODERNITY

In the history of the Mexican modern, Juan O'Gorman (1905–82) is remembered as the architect who built some of the country's first functionalist projects, along with his mentor José Villagrán García, as well as creating the iconic murals of the University Library in Mexico City (UNAM). Oddly enough, Villagrán and O'Gorman represent two separate tropes of functionalism in the 1930s, with Villagrán concerned more with its aesthetic aspect, and O'Gorman fervently promoting its rational and constructional aspect.[14] By the age of 19, O'Gorman had already read Le Corbusier's *Vers une Architecture* and dreamt of applying Le Corbusier's ideas for the house as a machine to live in, to his own projects. Opportunity was not far off; in the 1930s O'Gorman built a series of houses in Mexico City, such as the house for Frances Toor (1935), for his brother Tomás (1931) and his own first house

(1932), in which many elements of Le Corbusier's architectural language of the period can be found.[15]

O'Gorman embraced functionalism's social ideals concerning maximum efficiency for minimum effort and, consequently, cost. This was to be achieved through mass production in housing and building infrastructure, which had to offer Mexican people a better chance primarily in education and living. As chief of the Building Department of the Secretariat of Public Education (SEP),[16] O'Gorman managed to materialise his ideas, building, in the space of 10 years (from 1932 to 1942), 25 new schools, extensions in eight existing buildings and repair works in another 20. His budget was equal to the amount of money used under the neo-colonial regime, some 10 years earlier, for a single school complex. O'Gorman was criticised for the rudimentary character of his schools, which were focused on covering basic needs, even though he did try to bring some variety into the scheme, by painting exterior façades in red, blue, pink, brown and green and in some cases commissioning murals for the interiors.[17]

Nevertheless, O'Gorman, much like Luis Barragán, abandoned functionalism soon after completing his activity in school building, quick to perceive that excessive glazed surfaces were not compatible with the Mexican climate. Additionally, the style was rapidly adopted by developers and speculators and became conveniently a-local. Thus, O'Gorman departed in search for his own personal idiom, first through muralist and (sur)realist painting. In fact, the life work of Juan O'Gorman and his restless and rebellious spirit can be 'justified' by a schism between painting and architecture, which for him is absolute during the interwar period, where he understands architecture mainly as engineering work committed to providing primarily for the basic needs of the people.[18]

In 1949, O'Gorman built another house for himself, after almost a decade of distancing himself from the architectural profession and having abandoned practice. This work was born from the merging of modern construction techniques and materials with morphological elements, colours and textures originating both in the colonial and pre-colonial past of Mexico. He declared it:

unfortunate that Le Corbusier, and not Frank Lloyd Wright, caught our attention [in the years of his architectural studies, author's note]. Wright would have helped us to stay closer to our true American tradition. ... His house, Taliesin, ... has a recognizable Mexican character. It revives the Meso-American tradition. It was Wright, a frequent visitor to our archaeological sites, who understood organic architecture as related to the human being in his geographical and historical content.[19]

In accordance with Wright's teachings about the merging of architecture with the land and the natural setting into which it is integrated, the house also features a merging between local materials (the lava stone) and industrialised, modern construction techniques (use of reinforced concrete and metal-framed windows). The house (Figure 4.2) was for O'Gorman an attempt at 'organic architecture', born from a cave in the volcanic land of San Ángel, which hosted the house's main living space, around which the rest of the rooms were arranged.[20] Mosaics made of the typical, native, dark-coloured stone covered most of the house's interior as well as exterior walls. Wright himself visited the house and congratulated O'Gorman on his work. The house descended directly from the aesthetic strand, so close to Mayan constructions, of four projects embodying Wright's experimentations with patterned concrete blocks.[21] Among these are the Alice Millard ('La Miniatura') and the Charles Ennis houses, both built between 1923 and 1924, in California.

It was the mosaic panels he designed for the exterior walls of the University Library in the new campus of the National Autonomous University of Mexico (UNAM) in Mexico City (1950–51) that earned O'Gorman international acclaim (Figure 4.3). They cover all four sides of the library tower (as high as ten storeys), which was initially planned in the form of Meso-American truncated pyramids. Rich in colours and covering a total surface of 4,400 square yards, the mosaics are made up of small stones each measuring less than two inches in diameter. They decorate the tower of closed stacks, which sits on the two almost completely glazed floors of reading rooms at the bottom. According to O'Gorman, mosaics 'bring us into the realm of colour as a part of architecture, which in antiquity and until the Renaissance was an essential part of the composition. It has been our good

FIGURE 4.2 Juan O'Gorman, the architect's house, San Ángel, Mexico City, 1949.

fortune, in Mexico, to initiate the movement to reincorporate painting and sculpture into architecture.'[22] He fervently admired works such as Antoni Gaudí's, whose mosaics 'reveal the love of decoration which is the beneficent characteristic of the baroque, and incidentally is inherent in our Mexican tradition.'[23]

FIGURE 4.3 Juan O'Gorman, University Library mosaic panels, National Autonomous University of Mexico, Mexico City, 1950–51.

Completed after World War II, the technique of the mosaics had nevertheless been developed by O'Gorman during the interwar period. According to O'Gorman, it was developed 'accidentally' while working on Anahuacali, Diego Rivera's studio-house-museum of Ancient Mexican Sculpture in San Pablo Tepetlapa, Mexico City, in 1945–6. The University Library murals were made from prefabricated slabs of a surface of about one square yard, and about two inches thick, in which a layer of coloured stone chips had been embedded before casting the reinforced concrete. Each slab featured a part of the overall design and could be easily lifted and assembled in situ on the building's façade.

Mural paintings had been present in the work of Mexican painters José Clemente Orozco, Diego Rivera and David Alfaro Siquieros since the early 1920s. These painters had worked together in the construction of the Ministry of Education building (Mexico City, 1920–21).[24] The building was commissioned by the revolutionary Minister José Vasconcelos (1921–4) and built in less than a year by the engineer Federico Méndez Rivas. Vasconcelos believed in the educational value of the murals for the Mexican people to transcend materialism in favour of spiritual values. Although the building itself responded mostly to a mix of colonial and neoclassical features, it highlights the fact, as Valerie Fraser points out, that the modernisation of the visual arts in Mexico and the break with the immediate past styles came about firstly through painting and more specifically muralism. Orozco, Rivera and Alfaro Siquieros were all partisans for an 'authentic' local language which would spring through new forms of painting while respecting Mexican tradition.[25] Similarly, the University Library's murals tell the story of modern Mexico as the culmination of both its pre-Hispanic and colonial past. They provide an illustrated account of Mexico's defeated Aztec emperor and the new imposed morality of the Spanish Catholic Church on the north and south walls, while depicting the history of modern Mexico and the Revolution on the west and east (shorter) façades.

In a 1967 publication regrouping the work of O'Gorman, Max Cetto, Matthias Goeritz, Luis Barragán, Felix Candela and Mario Pani, Villagrán addressed the way the 'Western culture' of that time mostly perceived Mexico as an 'other', exotic (if not 'barbaric') world that needed the West's savoir faire,[26] and talked of a generation of architects expressing themselves in construction with a distinctive Mexican accent[27] that at the same time appears to be 'occidental'. Mexico's ties with 'Western culture' have, in reality, always been close due to its colonial past: 'In the University City, the Library, with its external murals, and the Stadium are two magnificent examples of this accent, because of the treatment of stone, of color, of textures and volumes.'[28]

MURALS AND THE BRAZILIAN MODERN

Murals equally marked the emergence of a characteristically local expression of modernity in Brazil, in one of the country's happiest moments of architectural history. In this instance, it was a wall clad with azulejos, the traditional Portuguese ceramic, tin-glazed tiles, created originally by the Arabs to imitate Byzantine and Roman mosaics. The work of the Brazilian painter Cândido Portinari, this ornate wall, with its hand-painted azulejos, was the first impression of the St Francis of Assisi Chapel (the Capela da Pampulha; Figure 4.4) that the visitor could gain from the street, as the building turned its back on the main access route to open onto a transition space next to the artificial lake, on the opposite side. Small ceramic tiles also covered the chapel's parabolic vaults as well as the interior curvilinear wall framing the baptistery. The chapel was the work of Oscar Niemeyer (1907–2012), who completed it in 1942, as part of a series of buildings commissioned by the Mayor of Belo Horizonte. The city was the new capital of the Minas Gerais province and the complex of buildings was part of an (eventually unsuccessful) effort to boost a suburban development around the Pampulha lake, in the north part of the city. The Casa do Baile, the Iate Club (Yacht Club) and the Casino (the first building of the group to be completed) in Belo Horizonte established Niemeyer as the figurehead of the Brazilian, free-form modern.

It was in the Casa do Baile (1942; Figure 4.5) that Niemeyer used for the first time the free-form, curvilinear canopy that characterises many of his subsequent works. The metaphor of the *mulata* woman that he used for his free-flowing forms epitomises his ornate, organic designs that recreate for Europeans and North Americans alike the myth of the sensual, exotic and mysterious Brazil. This was the essence of a new type of modern, one that was reinvented to adapt to the unique cultural and historical blend of the Brazilian people. Ornamentation

FIGURE 4.4 (*opposite*) Oscar Niemeyer, Capela da Pampulha, Belo Horizonte, 1942.

FIGURE 4.5 Oscar Niemeyer, Casa do Baile, Pampulha, Belo Horizonte, 1942.

here emerges as an inherent characteristic of the Brazilian modern, which is established through the trope of continuity with Brazil's colonial Baroque art (*see also* Chapter 1).

This continuity is above all apparent in stone and ceramic (with azulejos or *pastilhas* – small tiles) cladding of different parts of the building and in latticework of various types, from the trellis used for shading the private verandas of the duplex suites of the Ouro Preto Grande Hotel[29] to Lúcio Costa's pre-cast ceramic grilles of the apartment blocks at the Parque Eduardo Guinle (Rio de Janeiro, 1948–54),[30] and the monumental scale of the perforated, white-painted concrete blocks of Olavo Redig de Campos at the Walther Moreira Salles residence, built in Rio de Janeiro in 1948–51 (Figure 4.6).[31] Redig de Campos was educated at Sapienza University in Rome. A member also of the Heritage Conservation Service at the Brazilian Foreign Ministry, he reconciles in his Walther Moreira Salles residence classical references (the organisation of the plan around a central patio and a monumental entrance with two marble columns set against a wall painted in an earthy red tone and inspired by the Pompeiian Villa of Mysteries) with elements of the mainstream modern (big glazed surfaces, a brise-soleil for sun protection and an inspired tropical landscape design by Roberto Burle Marx).

The Capela da Pampulha was not the first time that azulejos had been used in Brazilian modern buildings: they had already marked the iconic building of the Ministry of Education and Public Health (MESP), in Rio de Janeiro.[32] The building scheme of the Ministry was initiated with a competition that took place in 1935 and was won by a classical, Art Deco-inspired design,[33] although this was never built. Instead, the commission was trusted to Lúcio Costa (a favourite with the regime) and a team of young architects, among them Oscar Niemeyer, Affonso Eduardo Reidy and Roberto Burle Marx, while Le Corbusier himself acted as design consultant. The MESP building was the first materialisation in Brazil of Le Corbusier's Five Points of a New Architecture: free plan and façade, *pilotis*, a roof garden and horizontal windows. Le Corbusier's contribution has led to some controversy as to the building's authorship in the years following the building's completion.[34] It was on his suggestion that azulejos cladding was used on external walls for protection and decoration. The building also featured a

FIGURE 4.6 (*opposite*) Olavo Redig de Campos, Walther Moreira Salles residence, Rio de Janeiro, 1948–51.

FIGURE 4.7 Cândido Portinari, mural, MESP building, Rio de Janeiro, 1945.

brise-soleil northern façade, and murals by Cândido Portinari (Figure 4.7) on the entrance plaza, the children's playroom and the auditorium. Portinari was in fact commissioned to produce 12 fresco murals in total.[35] Measuring 11 square feet each, the finished murals offered visual representations of the nation's most important natural products: wood, sugar cane, cattle, gold mining, yerba maté, coffee, iron, rubber, cotton and tobacco. The special attention Portinari pays to the human figures of his pieces, evident also in his extensive portrait work, reflects both his own past in Brazil's coffee fields and the country's multiracial origins.[36]

FIGURE 4.8 Gio Ponti, in collaboration with Emilio Lanza, Torre Rasini, Milan, 1933, balcony detail.

Portinari's artwork embodied in the best possible way a turn in Brazil's history, from its conservative, post-colonial past to a progressive future based on the robust, rural potential of the country and represented by modern aesthetics. The MESP building was commissioned by Getúlio Vargas' government, which came into power in 1930 and was initially sympathetic to fascism. Thus, in some ways, the contradiction of a right-wing regime which to a point allies with the modern to promote nationalistic concepts, greatly resembles the role Mussolini played in establishing modern aesthetics in interwar Italy.

MILANESE DESIGN EXUBERANCE

Framed against the social and political role of modernity, ornamentation could not be excluded by the Mexican or Brazilian modern. Much in the same way, it could not be omitted from the work of Italian moderns and their classical tradition, especially because many of them were as active in the field of industrial, furniture and product design as they were in the architectural arena. The easy affinity that the international modern was finding, in the first quarter of the 20th century, with building developers amid a rising bourgeoisie (and which led O'Gorman to abandon functionalism) was the driving force behind the exceptional work of Milanese architects. They focused on a unified design scheme merging architecture with decorative arts and interior furnishing, in many cases produced in mass scale.

Gio Ponti was one of those architects already building, since the beginning of the century, for a well-to-do, upcoming middle class, for which modern design was acting as a symbol of lifestyle and status. In this first quarter of the century, his work was still largely sympathetic to the Novecento movement, which proposed both the return of Italian art to the celebrated principles of its classical past and its renewal. The Torre Rasini building, in Milan (1933; Figure 4.8), a collaboration with Emilio Lanza, brings together 'the two dominant architectural styles of the 1930s: the streamlined modernism inspired by Rationalist principles, and the more moderate Novecento style characterized by diverse materials, massing and traditional elements.'[37] Equally, a decorative intention on the architect's part, as well as attention to the building's finishing details, can be read on the façade (as well as in the interior) in parallel with a rationalist logic. The decorative intention is evident

FIGURE 4.9 Gio Ponti, Palazzo Montecatini, Milan, 1936.

in the marble and travertine facing of the building, in the diamond patterns on the underside and the metallic handrails of the balconies, while the rationalist logic is seen in the stepped terraces of the top floors, which accentuate the block's height. This is a typical high-rise solution with Ponti and endows the building with a roof terrace that unfortunately has not been used as the architect aspired, despite the Mediterranean-style awnings and the pergolas he designed.

For Ponti, the details of the Rasini high-rise housing are an early example of his decorative vein, which is fully manifested in his post-war projects and the industrial design of ceramic tiles used for cladding entire volumes[38] and decorating interior spaces, often through alternating limited decorative sequences and modules. It is also discernible even in clearly functionalist buildings of the interwar period, of which the famous Palazzo Montecatini (executed in two separate phases, the first one in 1936 and the second post-war, in 1951) is perhaps the most representative example. Ponti's Palazzo Montecatini (Figure 4.9) established a new landmark for the city of Milan and contributed to inventing a new paradigm in the history of architecture as 'everything inside the building had to be invented from scratch: the new typology [*author's note:* of an office building] required new objects, new materials'.[39] The Palazzo Montecatini features a sleek volume and austere façade, in a concave shape (completed with the execution of the second commission) which highlights its rationalist logic, especially when compared with the eclectic design of the first headquarters of the company that commissioned the Palazzo Montecatini. (This first headquarters was built on a neighbouring plot, on the same street, in 1926, only 10 years earlier than Ponti's project.) The continuous rhythm of the windows reflects the regularity of the arrangement of the desks inside. The dimensions of the office desk were here used as a module for the arrangement of the interior spaces. Still, in the smooth appearance of the building's front, which is clad with marble and where the windows run flush (without sills) with the panelling, Ponti's inventiveness and ornamental taste can be noticed in the visual effect accomplished by cutting the *cipollino*-type marble of the façade against the grain.[40]

Ponti's designs evoke a taste for elegance and comfort in life, running from the light, Italian-style awnings of the roof terrace of the Laporte House (Milan, 1935–6)

FIGURE 4.10 Gio Ponti, Villa Planchart, Caracas, 1954–55.

to the overhead lighting system of the Lerici Italian Cultural Institute (Stockholm, 1952–8), which highlights the honeycomb-shaped slab, designed in collaboration with the engineer Pier Luigi Nervi.[41] Ponti believed in design as a unified whole, encompassing all aspects of a building's functioning. This could become true thanks to the uniquely close relationships that he developed, in many cases, with his clients. One typical example is the villa that he designed in Caracas, Venezuela, in 1954–5 for the collectors Anala and Armando Planchart (Figure 4.10), where Ponti fully furnished and decorated the interior space, with works both of Italian and of local artists. Decorative geometric patterns on the ceiling were in this instance matched with the colours and patterns of the furniture and of the protective screens designed for the indoor windows looking onto the double-height living space of the villa.[42]

It would seem as if, with Italian designers like Ponti, geometric and material-originated decorative patterns applied on the interior (and sometimes exterior) surfaces of floors, walls and ceilings were almost spontaneous. This is something to be observed especially after World War II in the work of architects such as Luigi Caccia Dominioni, who despite clearly rationalist façades create, through the use of floor mosaics, a unique fusion between the flows of human activity in the interior of buildings and the geometry of the layout. This aspect of Caccia Dominioni's work is examined more in detail in Chapter 5.

In the Brazilian and Mexican forefront of modernity, ornamentation was inherently connected with architecture's social and cultural meaning. It was also closely linked with the use of locally sourced materials and traditional techniques that were being reinvented in the construction process. The kind of holistic treatment of the building as a uniformly decorated, simple geometric box that O'Gorman applies in the UNAM Library building finds its aesthetic continuity in the relatively early work of the Swiss architects Herzog & De Meuron, such as their Dominus Winery, in Napa Valley, California (1995–8) or their Prada Store in Tokyo (2003). In the Dominus Winery, the structural material (locally sourced basalt encased in gabions, which are more or less densely filled in different parts of the building to regulate aeration and light) automatically becomes the building's decorative skin. Although both examples can hardly find any parallels with the social context and historical conjunctions that defined the Mexican modern, they partially refer to the same conceptual concern that seeks to identify the building's function and social role with its envelope. In the following chapter, discussion will focus on transitions between exterior and interior, and the perception of space by the user moving between these two.

CHAPTER 5
GEOMETRY AND SPATIAL EXPERIENCE

This chapter looks at an alternative tradition of the modern, associated with explorations of the organic, which is demonstrated in the use of irregular geometry and unique spatial forms. Discussion here focuses mainly on the formal geometry that could be characterised as organic, and its impact on the spatial experience of the user, through emphasis placed on the visual perception of space. It is an architecture centred on the individual user, generated from plans tailored around the user's functional needs and movements, from the interior to the exterior. This design approach is particularly relevant in the present era, where new technological advancements linked with digitally produced design, construction methods and materials enable the generation of free forms and buildings unhindered by the constraints of Euclidean geometry.

THE FLOWING SPACE

For Frank Lloyd Wright, one of the first architects to use the term 'organic' for his work,[1] the organic is associated with plastic, fluent, coherent forms and the 'natural use of nature-materials or synthetics, and appropriate methods of construction.'[2] In his 1945 book, *Towards an Organic Architecture*,[3] Bruno Zevi questioned rationalism, as well as its classical roots, while announcing, in the post-war era, a tendency and an imminent need for a more humane architecture. He defined the organic through paradigms of dynamic forms and the architecture's social role in the creation of a truly democratic society.

Discussing Alvar Aalto's Villa Mairea (Noormarkku, 1937–9; Figure 5.1), Alan Colquhoun describes how the wooden poles (whether structural or decorative) that Aalto uses to divide the single living space of the house into different zones, 'become metonyms for the pine forest'. According to Colquhoun, this building of Aalto's, 'with its abruptly juxtaposed elements and its metaphors of nature, was a radical departure from the linear logic of the New Objectivity.'[4] The free forms found in the pool, the balconies, the entrance canopy, the boundaries marking the passing from one material or from one space unit to another, as well as the project's spatial organisation in general, reflect a distance from a regularity often found in views and perspectives. The house's volumes are interlocking and assembled in plan in such a way as to create a protected, central outdoor space; oblique, elongated views reveal and enhance the project's depth in space while blurring the boundaries of

FIGURE 5.1 Alvar Aalto, Villa Mairea, Noormarkku, Finland, 1937–39, interior view.

the interior with the exterior. Juhani Pallasmaa talks of Aalto's 'flowing space' which is 'associated with the limitless space of nature' and points out that 'in addition to their organic associations the irregular intervals of units create strong continuity from one space or situation to the next.'[5]

In a similar way, Wright created space *continuos* by setting the building's sub-volumes into one another. Wright's articulated spaces established an ambiguity between interior and exterior, between entirely open to one another and completely separated units.[6] This ambiguity culminated in the iconic Fallingwater (Bear Run, Pennsylvania, 1935–7), where the interior of the house blends organically with the

GEOMETRY AND SPATIAL EXPERIENCE

exterior, through a dynamic overlapping of the man-made and the natural scenery. The articulation of the project's sub-spaces, of solids and voids, is one feature of Wright's work that has been put forward by several historiographers of the modern, as well as by the architect himself, as a quality of organic design.[7] Henry-Russell Hitchcock talks of rooms flowing into one another, to describe Wright's revolutionary approach to the individual house, an approach he was using from the beginning of the 20th century.[8] Vincent Scully discusses the 'constantly fluid spatial quality' of Wright's projects as a characteristic of modern architecture in general.[9] Wright himself refers in his *Testament* to a new space dimension (depth-dimension)[10] and his concept of space based on the moving viewer, which connects him with the work of Cubist painters. Oblique views penetrate the interconnected spaces and enhance the sensation of a deep space in his buildings.

ARCHITECTURAL PROMENADE AND SPATIAL DEPTH

Sharing similarities with Wright's compositional logic is Le Corbusier's concept of the *promenade architecturale*, which is materialised for the first time in La Roche House (Paris, 1923–5). The term *promenade architecturale* only appears as such in Le Corbusier's writings from 1929,[11] in the first volume of his *Œuvre Complète*, precisely to describe the La Roche House project. The essential components of the architectural promenade consist of: the use of various architectural devices to raise the visitor's curiosity to explore the entire space of a project; the creation of various successive viewpoints that allow visitors to discover the space from different angles; and finally, the visual relation between separate space units and the building as a whole, from each of these vantage points.

The concept of the architectural promenade makes apparent the influence that Picasso and Cubism had on Le Corbusier. Cubism broke with traditional representational logics and perspective principles dating from the Renaissance, which strictly divided the canvas into foreground and background planes, to dissect the object of study and offer in the same snapshot various facets of it, which would not normally all be visible from a single angle. In the same sense, arriving from a meandering trail through the garden to La Roche House, one reaches a triple-height entrance hall, situated between the house and the studio gallery. A balcony protruding in space, as well as the limited views of the upper levels enabled by the entrance void and simultaneously revealed to the visitor, lead to a vertically arranged sequence of different vantage points. These are carefully planned in order to sequentially uncover the entire space of the house while at the same time modifying the visitor's perception of the central hall. The promenade often entails the elongation of the visitor's path in space, which culminates in the expressive curve of the studio ramp. Leading from the first-floor gallery to the library of the upper floor, the ramp connects the house's distinct zones, offering a chance to admire the displayed paintings from shifting viewpoints while at the same time gradually gaining sight of the rest of the house's interior.

In a 1978 publication edited by Bruno Zevi, Edward Frank explains the difference between the designs of Le Corbusier and those of Frank Lloyd Wright, when it comes to a project's spatial depth:

> *To the Corbusian symbol of the man with the lifted arm who occupies space, Wright counterposes the moving man that cleaves space. With Le Corbusier, emphasis is on the vertical, on man and architecture that challenge gravity; with Wright, instead, it is on the horizontal, on space and man flowing and moving on the surface of the earth.*[12]

Wright employed diagonal axes in order to open up the plan and bring a new depth in his projects, breaking up symmetry, although not orthogonality (at least, not until the post-war, last phase in his career), eliminating corners and creating staggered volumes, offering oblique, dynamic, extended views by 'stretching' the interior into the exterior. This is a characteristic most evident in his Prairie-style houses, such as the Robie House, built as early as 1907–10 in Chicago (Figure 5.2).[13]

Le Corbusier's occasional curves and free-form planning in his pre-World War II architectural production is linked with the architectural promenade but also with the opening up of the interior towards the exterior, enabling a panorama of vision, thus liberating the human eye from traditional Beaux Arts enfilades. The free forms of the ground floor and the roof terrace of the Villa Savoye (1928) find references in machinist aesthetics and at the same time, strangely enough, with a poetic element in architecture (which was often rapidly dismissed in critiques of the modern

FIGURE 5.2 Frank Lloyd Wright, Robie House, Chicago, 1907–10.

and its mass-scale buildings during the 1970s). This last element is evoked in a purposefulness and perfect fit, characteristic of industrially engineered objects. However, it should be noted that the Cubist superimposition of planes (interior and exterior) through the extended glazed surfaces of the building envelope are radically different from a processional planning which is found in the essence of the architectural promenade and which culminates in the architecture of the organic as heralded by Bruno Zevi.

BREAKING UP WITH TRADITIONAL VIEWPOINTS

In *Towards an Organic Architecture* (1945), Zevi discussed the paradigms of both Wright and of Aalto.[14] The book advocated the departure from rigid interpretations of modernist aphorisms (perhaps needed in the first phase of dissemination of the modern, but never actually applied, even by their own authors).[15] Zevi talked of an architecture of movement and a dynamic quality, which he took caution to distinguish from 'biological or anthropomorphic' fallacies, found 'at the root of expressionism'.[16] Expressionism has been described, in the context of the German modernity of the 1920s, also as 'functionalism' and opposed to the 'rationalist' strand of the Neue Sachlichkeit (New Objectivity).[17] Thus, the functionalists, such as Erich Mendelsohn, Bruno and Max Taut, Hugo Häring or Hans Scharoun (Figures 5.3 and 5.4), were in search of an architecture of a unique form, both dependent on and expressive of its interior functions, while the rationalists, around Walter Gropius and the Bauhaus school, were seeking typical solutions and forms that could easily be repeated.[18] In this sense, the house that Bruno Taut built for himself in Dahlewitz, Berlin, in 1926, on a quasi-triangular layout (with a convex side containing the entrance) mainly answers a concern for a less conventional response of the building to its setting, by adopting a uniquely shaped layout. However, Taut also achieves a multiplicity of views and orientations through the way the radial geometry of the layout is tackled, while assigning separate spaces to every function.

Equally, the paradigms that Zevi highlights in *Towards an Organic Architecture* often deviate from the right angle and are additionally inspired by natural forms. However, in the light of the social meaning that Zevi attaches to architecture, which aspires to the formation of a democratic society where architecture holds man as its protagonist instead of the object-building, the divergence from the orthogonal grid is not to be sought in formal irregularities and the building's outline, but, perhaps most importantly, in the dynamic unravelling of the interior space. This happens in close relation to the needs of its users and a search for unique spatial experiences. After all, the modern and its precursors (such as expressionism) are fundamentally connected with radical alterations of the concept of vision that broke up with traditional (Renaissance) perspective views and dominant viewpoints.

FIGURE 5.3 Hans Scharoun, Baensch House, Spandau, Berlin, 1936, plan.

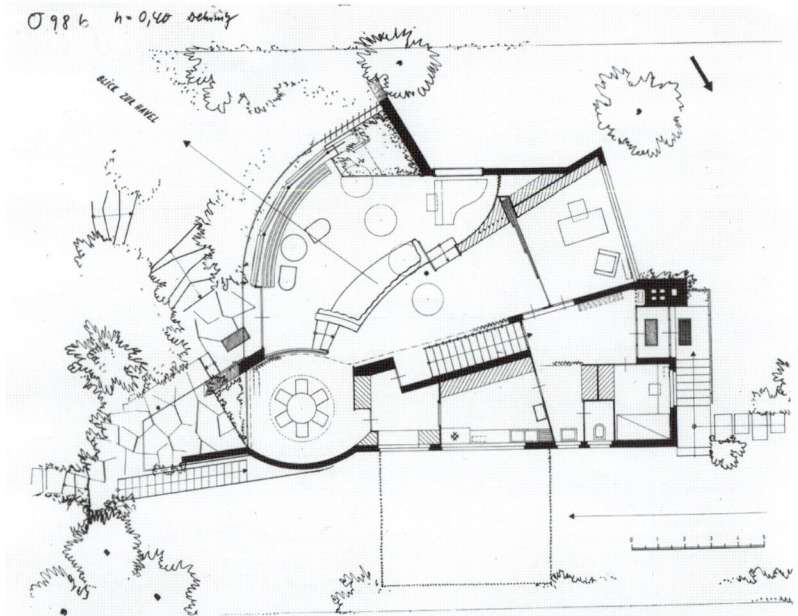

FIGURE 5.4 Hans Scharoun, Baensch House, Spandau, Berlin, 1936, interior view.

Peter Blundell Jones talks of 'aperspectivity' as a design quality found in Hans Scharoun's work, especially his post-World War II production, such as the unbuilt project for the Gerd Rosen art gallery, which he characteristically connects with an act of social meaning: 'For Scharoun, escape from the dominant central axis and symmetry was an escape from both aristocratic and fascist power, leading to a democratic situation where people were permitted equal but diverse points of view, both literally and metaphorically.'[19] Scharoun's layouts are not dominated by preferences for viewpoints that would provide ideally framed shots of the interior space, as happens in the case of other masters of the modern. His free-form, curvilinear interiors and diagonal arrangements of flowing space can thus be represented in photographic shots only by skewed angles and cut-off frames. In the same spirit as Wright's work, Scharoun's dynamic spaces can be fully experienced only by moving viewers in four-dimensions (space and time).

CONSTRUCTING VISUAL SEQUENCES

Although built a lot later than Scharoun's house in Spandau, the house of the German/Mexican architect Max Cetto in Mexico City (1949) offers a similar experience of 'processual' reading of space through the pathways leading to the house (Figures 5.5 and 5.6). The form of the house works here in close conjunction with the particularity of the site and the unique rocky landscape. The first house to be built in the Pedregal housing development, in which Cetto worked together with Luis Barragán on various single-family homes, Cetto's house is located in a patch of land of uneven topography. The architect placed the initially single-storey residence at the highest point of the plot, without foundations. The building is a mixed construction and an early expression of a specific, Mexican regionalist idiom, with lava-stone walls that are partly load-bearing for the concrete slabs. The particularity of the project lies also in its functional configuration: the house consists of two parts, developed in contrasting geometries. The main section comprises living and sleeping rooms, as well as an office space, and follows a strictly rectilinear geometry. The remaining spaces include the kitchen, a courtyard and a playroom for Cetto's three daughters that all follow the land's contour, adopting a sinuous form and skewed interior partitions. The free forms of this part of the house can be read in concurrence with its garden, which was arranged by the architect's wife: left as far as possible to its natural state, it includes native plants from all parts of Mexico. The water tower dominates the joint point of the

FIGURE 5.5 Max Cetto, the architect's house, Pedregal, Mexico City, 1949, steps leading to the main entrance.

FIGURE 5.6 Max Cetto, the architect's house, Pedregal, Mexico City, 1949, view from the garden.

two sections of the house; a spiral staircase is also placed close to the water tower, to link the original ground level of the house with the upper floor, which was added later to provide space for a guest room and the architect's atelier.

An overall view of the house is offered from the west, when one stands relatively far from it, but as the visitor approaches, the rich vegetation, together with the meandering paths and staircases that take one to the main entrance, reveal only parts of the house from specific vantage points. Eventually the building's volume emerges as a surprise, at the end of the visitor's journey up the path. The adventure in the approach to the house, as well as the way in which the landscape is translated into form, is reminiscent of the German expressionism of the 1920s. Max Cetto had been taught by Hans Poelzig at the Technical School of Berlin and characteristically devoted the book he published in the 1960s about his work to his teacher.

Carefully constructed visual sequences that create an added theatricality to the spaces of everyday life are also in the centre of Gio Ponti's architectural work.

GEOMETRY AND SPATIAL EXPERIENCE

Ponti stated, 'We should never block the perspectives, we should make people see "more than they can", create enfilades, focal points, openings of light.'[20] Throughout his career, Ponti often used irregular geometry for interior walls or for his projects' exterior outlines. Straight pathways that are linked to a dominant perspective are rarely found in his projects. His sketches are often heavily marked with lines of vision (Figure 5.7), representing not only the most interesting views from various vantage points, but, most importantly, the way the spaces can be 'stretched'

FIGURE 5.7 Gio Ponti, An Ideal Small House, project, 1934.

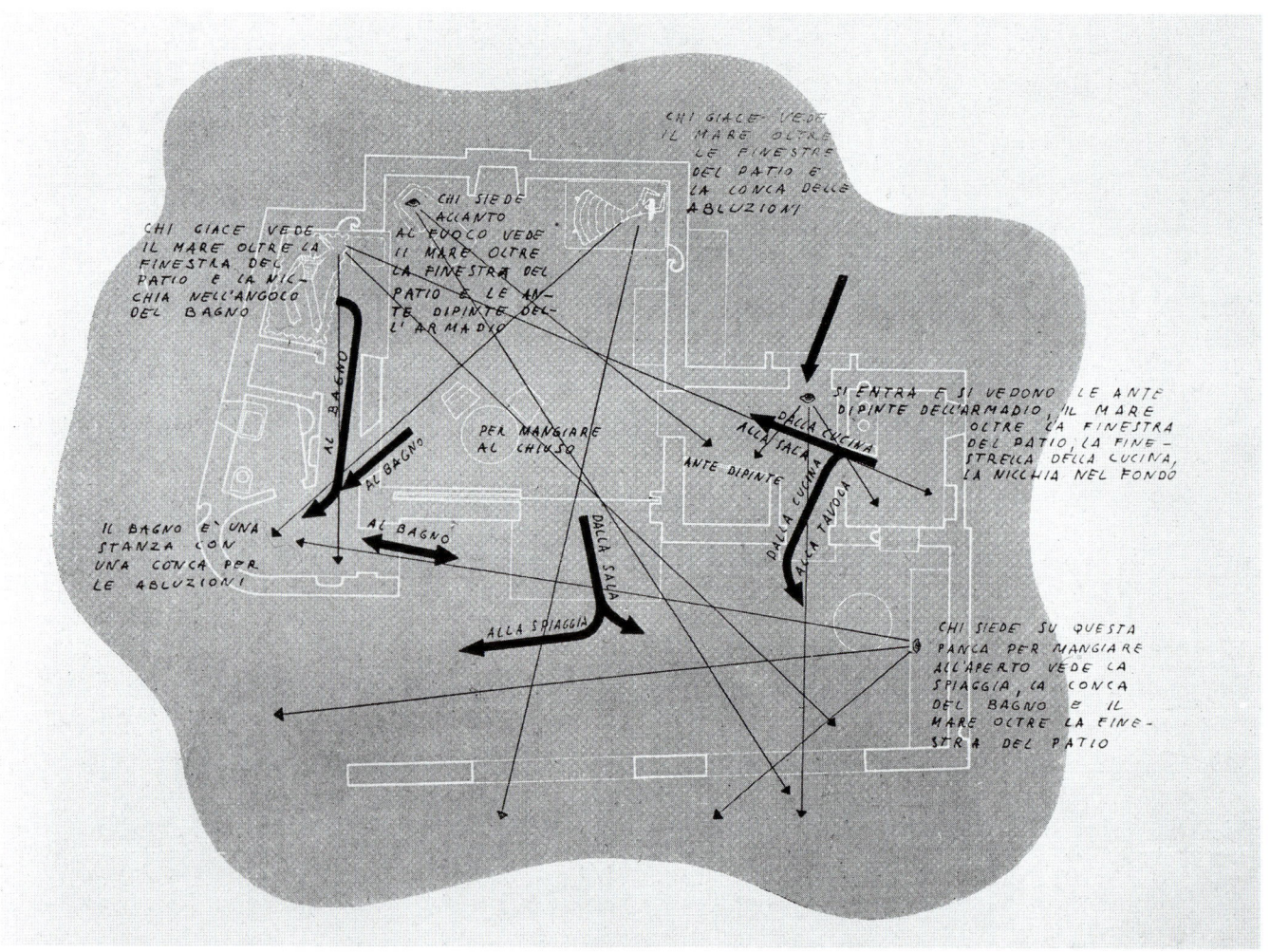

through the user's gaze towards specific directions of alternating range. As pointed out by the architect Rafael De Cáceres, 'With Gio Ponti, diagonal lines are not the result of the plan's geometry, but are born by the desire of dilating space, of converting it into a changing scenery.'[21]

Another architect linked to Ponti, with the same concern for a flowing unravelling of spatial events, from the interior to the exterior of his projects, is the Catalan José Antonio Coderch de Sentmenat. This time the spatial flow is achieved mostly through rectilinear geometry articulated in staggered volumes, which are typical of Coderch's personal style. Although 20 years younger than Ponti, Coderch owed the light cast on his work from the international press largely to Ponti, who often published in the pages of *Domus* (mostly after World War II, when he resumed his editorial position at the journal) several of Coderch's works. Both Ponti and Coderch seem to oscillate, throughout their careers, between their contemporary local and global context. They put emphasis, in various moments, on the international, a-contextual principles of modern architecture on the one hand, yet also on personal styles related to their national backgrounds.

Coderch's most well-known work, the apartment building Casa de la Marina (1952) in the area of the Barceloneta, Barcelona, is characterised by the skewed lines of the flats' interior partitions and the wooden brise-soleil that Coderch used for the first time in this project, but which later become typical of the angles in his buildings. Coderch's reasons for using this particular device were associated with the urban fabric; diagonal views avert the vis-à-vis monotony of homogeneously built, straight-lined fronts. The oblique lines of the flats' layout achieve a visual complexity and sense of enlarged space that would otherwise have been impossible in units of such exiguous dimensions.

Ugalde House (1951), in Caldes d'Estrac, Barcelona, is one of the few examples of Coderch's work that answers to a free geometry of curved outlines, and is strongly reminiscent of the work of Scharoun, with which Coderch was familiar. Coderch's Olano House (1957; Figure 5.8) and his unusual twin diamond-shaped layout is an illustrative example of the gradual unfolding of the morphology of the interior towards the exterior, eventually highlighting the uniqueness of the plot

FIGURE 5.8 José Antonio Coderch de Sentmenat, Olano House, Comillas, Spain, 1957, main floor plan.

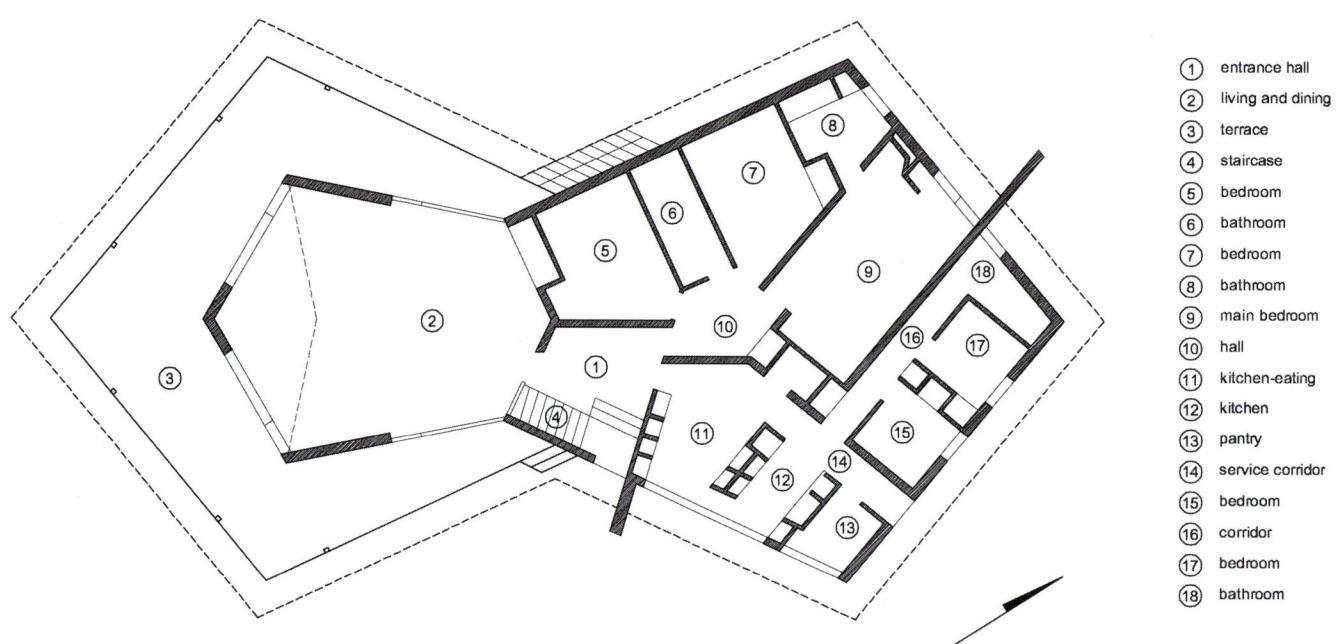

where the house is built. Situated on a river delta on the northern coast of Spain, the house opens up towards the best orientation, facing southeast towards the river. Instead of entirely dematerialising the diamond's angle, which points south, Coderch arranged the boundary of the living room, alternating solids and openings along contiguous edges. Thus, the viewer is drawn towards several unobstructed perspectives. The private part of the house is anchored to the land, in direct dialogue with the site's contour, while the communal part focuses on the water's flow. Evocatively, Coderch's work was also among those promoted by Zevi.[22]

CURATING MOVEMENT

The case of the Milanese architect Luigi Caccia Dominioni is still quite unknown to an international public. Usually mentioned in the Italian and Swiss bibliography as one of the architects that shaped the face of urban Milan in the post-World War II era, Dominioni enjoyed a particularly long career that spanned more than 70 years. His work (Figures 5.9 and 5.10) is characterised by complex spatial arrangements that place emphasis on intermediary spaces, such as corridors, halls and anterooms (along the lines of Baroque architecture, of which Dominioni was a fan) as well as on construction details. Dominioni's spatial flows are often also materialised in floor mosaics, through an impeccable decorative flair that brings to life sequences of interior and exterior views, particularly in residential spaces. Dominioni equally treats human movement in his domestic architecture as a staged event, as an adventure of a continuous flow and rounded-off changes of direction.[23]

This kind of design finds its equivalent in more recent projects and a rekindling of the organic that can be observed in the work of Swiss architects, both in terms of architectural and of urban planning. To mention only one example, the Volta Mitte development (Figures 5.11 and 5.12), by Christ & Gantenbein (Basel, 2005–10), is a five-storey, mixed-use building, presenting a typical straight-lined front of alternated brick and glass bands towards the city, while turning a 'deformed', playful back towards the inner courtyard of the urban block. This arrangement reflects a free treatment of the flats' interior space; no apartment is identical to another in layout but the central living space in all of them flows longitudinally and offers unhindered oblique views in different directions.

Such projects are generated by the designer's concern to create spaces centred around the user and the experience one acquires by moving around in space and by gradually discovering its depth and dimensions. This intention is materialised through geometry that deviates from the strictly orthogonal prisms characterising the volumetric compositions of the mainstream modern; but most importantly through concatenations of focal points and carefully constructed views in space. Research has often dwelled on the first component of this alternative strand of modernity, while a lot of room for study still exists in relation to the second.

FIGURE 5.9 Luigi Caccia Dominioni, floor layout of Via Vigoni 13, Milan, 1956–59.

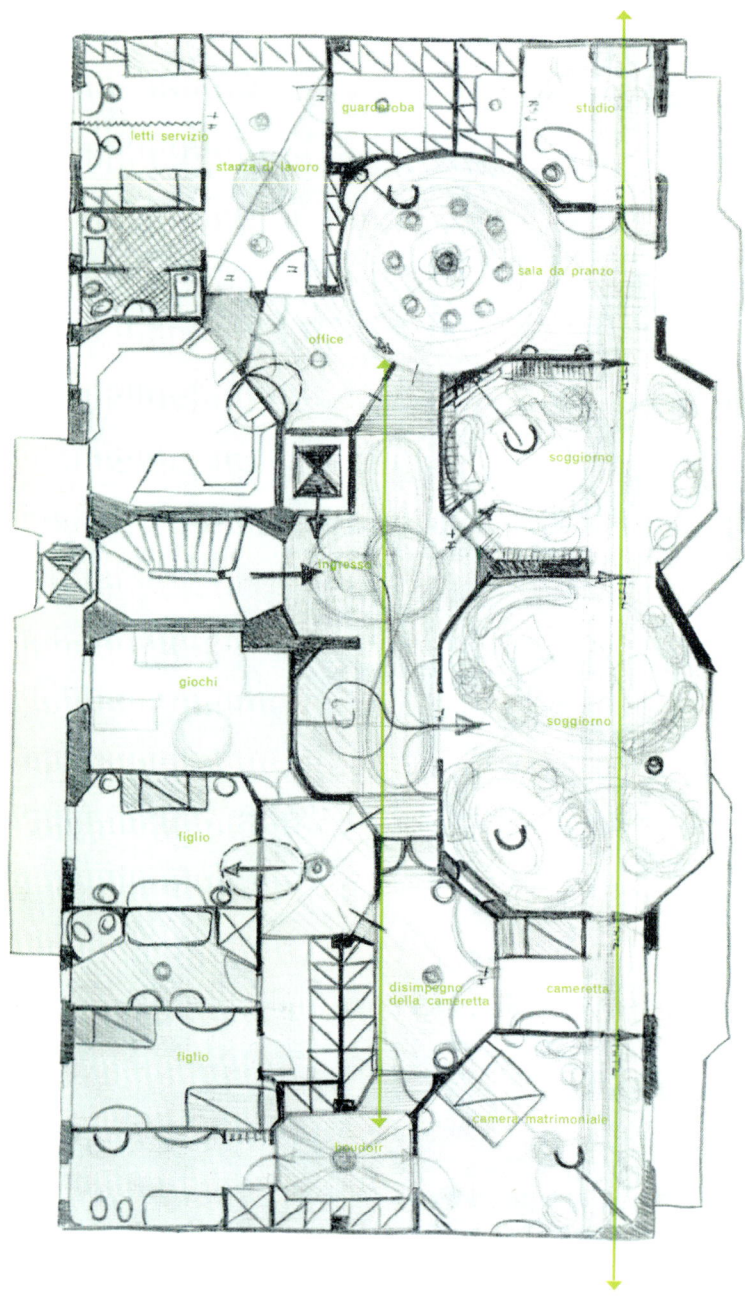

FIGURE 5.10 Luigi Caccia Dominioni, interior view of third-floor flat, Via Vigoni 13, Milan, 1956–9.

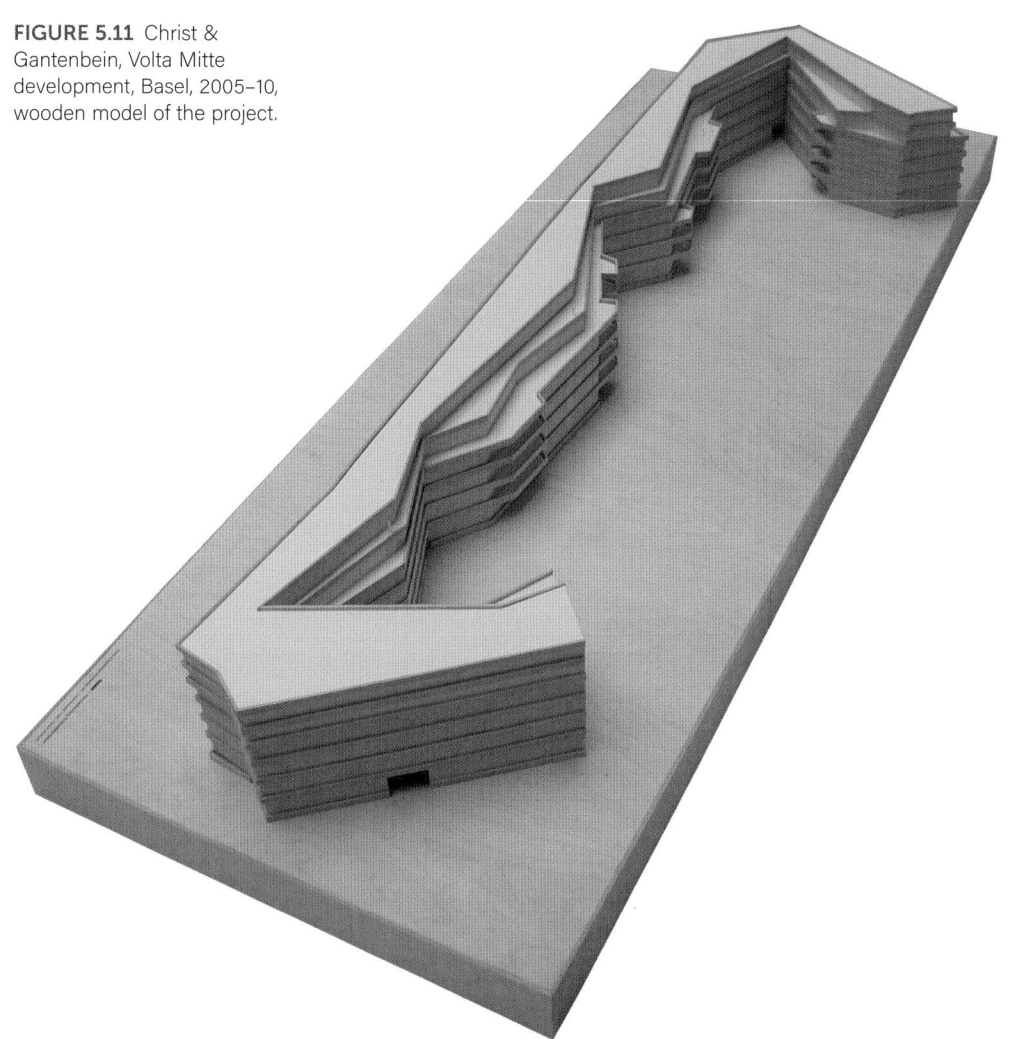

FIGURE 5.11 Christ & Gantenbein, Volta Mitte development, Basel, 2005–10, wooden model of the project.

The last part of the book returns to the connection between the mainstream and the alternative, by examining the work of architects who found themselves equally immersed in local and international approaches of modernity. Chapters 6 and 7 examine the diaspora of Continental architects and ideas in Latin America and Britain, two parts of the world closely linked with Continental Europe in terms of cultural influences, yet singled out by their own unique expressions of modernity.

FIGURE 5.12 Christ & Gantenbein, Volta Mitte development, 2005–10 interior view of a flat.

GEOMETRY AND SPATIAL EXPERIENCE

CHAPTER 6

THE MODERN DIASPORA: LATIN AMERICA

BY ANTIGONI KATSAKOU AND ILIANA MIRANDA-ZACARIAS

In January 1943, an exhibition about new Brazilian architecture entitled *Brazil Builds* opened at the Museum of Modern Art in New York under the curation of Philip Goodwin. The exhibition lasted only two months, moving immediately after New York to the Museum of Fine Arts in Boston, under the auspices of the Pan American Society. It was nevertheless the first of a series of events that explored the ways of the New Architecture in Latin American countries. In 1955, Henry-Russell Hitchcock curated another exhibition at the Museum of Modern Art in New York, entitled *Latin American Architecture since 1941*. He also authored an accompanying publication, arguing that the region had a lot to offer in examples of state-promoted architecture, such as housing and infrastructure building, that would 'shame' what had been done so far in the northern part of the Americas.[1] Equally, monographs such as Stamo Papadaki's *The Work of Oscar Niemeyer* (1950) would acquaint the public of North America and of Continental Europe with an architecture that was proving both kinship and independence from the sources of its inspiration. This was a version of the modern that carried within it the originality and true essence of an ingenuous, localised translation of its basic formal and functional principles. Interest in Latin American architecture was somewhat subdued during the last quarter of the 20th century, only to be rekindled recently in the spirit of a general re-evaluation of the breadth and scope of the modern across the globe.

This chapter discusses the impact of the European modern in Latin America by focusing on a few representative cases of architects and their projects in Mexico and Brazil. In these cases, as well as in Argentina, the modern was to a larger degree imported from Europe during the interwar period and divulged as a dominant current earlier than in other countries of Latin America, such as Colombia or Venezuela. In Argentina, the stylistic polyphony reigning in major urban centres of the country and the large production of architectural works focusing on neoclassical aesthetics makes the modern less relevant for the architectural evolution of the country in these first decades of the 20th century.

Apart from relevant publications in the general and specialist press, the import of ideas of the European modern to Latin American countries could be encapsulated in three main avenues: firstly, the visits that architects of the European avant-garde paid, often in pursuit of new commissions and with the goal of promoting the common cause for social change and a new, appropriate architectural language; secondly, through architects originating from the region, who spent their studies, a part of their training or the beginnings of their professional career in Europe and in ateliers of the avant-garde masters, before establishing themselves in their home countries; lastly, through a bulk of emigration that happened during the 1930s, mostly involving architects of Jewish origin or of progressive ideas, due to the coming to power of fascist regimes. It should nevertheless be noted here that European immigration was hardly a new phenomenon where Latin America was concerned. A wave of émigrés arrived in Argentina and Brazil at the turn of the 20th century in search of new opportunities; still, it was during the 1930s that Latin American countries became leading destinations for many European immigrants, due to adverse social and financial circumstances in their countries of origin.

THE AVANT-GARDE ON TOUR

Among those who visited Latin America to expand their business and influence, Le Corbusier is the most illustrative example. An excellent self-publicist dedicated to an intensive promotion of his work and concepts, he made several trips to Brazil (1929, 1936, 1962), Argentina (1929), Colombia (1947, 1949, 1950, 1951) and Uruguay (1929, on his way to Buenos Aires), giving lectures and building ties with professional and political groups, and actively pursuing new invitations and commissions. His influence was not always as noteworthy as his efforts. In Argentina, he was mostly an inspiration on a 'virtual' level through his writings and projects; the nine conferences that he gave in Buenos Aires in October 1929, invited by architects such as Victoria Ocampo and Alfredo González Garaño, went mostly unnoticed, despite his usual tactics of provocation.[2] His solutions were far too costly and irrelevant to his audience, although they reappeared in 1939 in urban planning proposals by the Argentinians Juan Kurchan and Jorge Ferrari Hardoy. These architects had worked at Le Corbusier's atelier during the previous year, along with the Catalan architect Antonio Bonet, who was instrumental in stirring young Argentinian architects towards the path of modernity.[3] The same thing happened with the two conferences Le Corbusier gave in Montevideo, where he was equally critical about the city's landmark buildings. The influence of Le Corbusier in these countries and perhaps in Latin America in general seems to have been mostly noteworthy in the post-World War II period through high-rise construction. This is similar, to a certain extent, with what happened in Britain, which will be discussed in more detail in Chapter 7.

Apart from Le Corbusier, there were also other significant architects and artists disseminating modern ideals through short-term visits. The novelist Filippo Tomasso Marinetti, founder of the futurist movement, visited Argentina (Buenos Aires, Cordoba, La Plata) in 1926, 15 years after the publication of his famous manifesto. Marcello Piacentini, chief architect of Mussolini's government, presented the work of Italian moderns in Argentina and Brazil in the first years of the 1930s, while he was invited as a consultant for the design of some federal buildings in Brazil.[4] The acquaintance of Argentinian architects with the work of Auguste Perret, which had been initiated with publications by Alberto Prebisch[5] in the magazine *Martín Fierro* in the mid-1920s,[6] was completed with his visit and the lectures that he gave there in 1936. The Italian-originated and Swiss-educated Alberto Sartoris, founding member of the CIAM and author of *Gli elementi dell'Architettura funzionale*,[7] also gave several talks in Latin American cities during the years 1935–6; the experience of those travels was recounted in his book *La Ciudad Moderna*, published in Cuba.[8] Similarly Josef Albers, the renowned Bauhaus professor, took the first of his many trips to Mexico in 1935, two years after emigrating to the USA.[9]

More importantly, although scarcely mentioned in the historiography of modern Brazilian architecture, Frank Lloyd Wright visited Rio de Janeiro in October 1931, to join the jury of the International Competition for the Columbus Lighthouse in Santo Domingo, at the request of the Pan-American Union of Architects, along with the Finnish architect Eliel Saarinen.[10] Wright spent almost a month in the city, giving lectures and receiving wide press coverage for his work. He was nevertheless treated with suspicion by the conservative architects of the Beaux Arts tradition, who were still dominating the National School of Fine Arts (ENBA) and who had recently overturned Lúcio Costa's appointment as Head of the School, by the newly established government of the commandant Getúlio Vargas.[11]

INFLUENCES AND INFLUENCERS

Regarding the training of Latin American architects in studios of the European avant-garde, again the case of Le Corbusier is the most prominent, with a long list of Latin Americans working under the architect as trainees or collaborating architects. The Colombians Rogelio Salmona and Germán Samper worked at his studio from 1948 to 1958 and from 1949 to 1954 respectively, while developing in collaboration the master plan of Bogotá (1948–51).[12] Naturally, this was a two-way influence. Le Corbusier was allegedly inspired for his Sarabhai House (Ahmedabad, India, 1951) and Jaoul House (Neuilly-sur-Seine, France, 1951) and their tile vaults, dating from the 1950s, by the newly built house of the Colombian architect Francisco Pizano de Brigard, which he discovered on one of his travels to Bogotá.[13]

The European architects who emigrated to Latin America during the 1930s mainly originated from Italy and Germany, although Austria and Poland were also affected, as was Spain. The Franco regime forced the exile of architects such as Josep Lluís Sert, who established himself in the USA with an intermediate stop in Paris (1937–9). Of this period, his most notable work is the Spanish Republic's pavilion at the World's Fair of 1937, which hosted Picasso's masterpiece *Guernica*.

Leopold Rother (1894–1978), a German originating from Breslau (in modern-day Poland), who emigrated to Colombia in 1936 and was naturalised in 1950, has been particularly influential for the conversion of the country's younger generation of architects towards modernity. Teaching at the National University of Colombia in Bogotá for 40 years (1938–78) and working for the State Building Department, the Dirección de Edificios Nacionales del Ministerio de Obras Públicas, at the beginning of his stay (1936–42), he produced the master plan for the Universidad Nacional de Colombia in Bogotá, at the end of the 1930s, a design strongly influenced by Bauhaus principles. By 1945, in the building for the University Press, he was mixing local artisanal materials with mass-produced ones, such as glass bricks used in large surfaces, while laying his plan out organically, around ramps, curved walls and spiral staircases.[14]

The Milanese Bruno Violi (1909–71), who succeeded Rother at the Dirección de Edificios Nacionales del Ministerio de Obras Públicas, after emigrating to Colombia in 1939 at the invitation of President Eduardo Santos, was equally important for Colombian modernity. He had worked with the Paris-based Swiss architect Denis Honegger, a pupil of Auguste Perret, on the Catholic University of Fribourg, one of Switzerland's most exceptional interwar buildings, with bare concrete façades. Violi introduced the pure white geometric prisms of the mainstream modern in his adopted home country, while focusing on a dynamic interplay of light and shadow in the design of the façade.[15]

Enrique Segarra Tomás (1908–88), a Spanish architect who emigrated to Mexico in 1940, was the 'common denominator' in all noteworthy private and public buildings of the 1940s, 1950s and 1960s in the city of Veracruz (Figure 6.1).[16] By the early 1940s, Veracruz was going through major transformations in a process of modernisation, and by the middle of the century the aesthetics of the New Architecture were proliferating in the city, although no architectural school existed until 1956. Segarra was one of the school's founders, while his practice, which gained a lot of its commissions from other Spanish nationals living in Veracruz, became a cradle for many generations of architects in the region.[17] Initially, Segarra worked as an employee of the company Eureka, which from 1942 oversaw the most ambitious programme of infrastructure construction carried out in the city during the 20th century. This included the modernisation of the port (at the time, the most important of the country), as well as many other public and private buildings.[18]

At the beginning of the 20th century there was an air of change breathing through Mexico and Brazil. The fresh chapter in their histories after independence from colonial regimes and the transition towards democracy through neo-colonial, liberal oligarchies, was celebrated by the adoption of the new aesthetics in architecture and the arts. The New Architecture not only reflected the technological progress that was promising equally impressive social advancements, but most importantly, it seemed able to embody the complex cultural identity of these new nations. Often, the new regimes were prepared to grant large-scale commissions to the avant-garde, as part of a desire to cut bonds with the past in a quest to affirm a new and unique local character, as well as a practical need to accommodate internal immigration, from rural communities to newly founded urban areas. Brasilia, the administrative capital of Brazil, designed by Lúcio Costa and Oscar Niemeyer, is the

FIGURE 6.1 Enrique Segarra Tomás, Cobos House, Veracruz, 1953.

most representative example of such an endeavour. Limited chances for projects of this extent were available in Europe.

BRAZIL'S NEW AESTHETICS

The influence of European architects was decisive in Brazil's first steps into the new aesthetics. Gregori Warchavchik is one such case. Russian-born, he was educated in Rome, where he also worked as an assistant to Marcello Piacentini. He moved to Brazil in 1923 and two years later published his Corbusian-influenced manifesto *Acerca de la Arquitectura Moderna* (On Modern Architecture), protesting against the academic eclecticism which continued to dominate the architectural stage of the country and thus drawing attention to his work. His marriage in 1927 to a Brazilian from a wealthy family and eventually his naturalisation may have facilitated his acceptance into São Paulo's upper class and secured him commissions.

In 1927–8, he built his own house in São Paulo, hailed as one of the first modern-style buildings in Brazil, which initially he had to adapt to the conservative views of the city's municipal services. Nevertheless, during construction, he managed to alleviate the project from many of its alien additions, such as friezes and conventional window frames.[19] This early example in Warchavchik's career is mostly the result of a formal research, focused on simple geometric volumes devoid from ornamentation. The new construction he completed in 1930 without a specific client in mind, in the São Paulo suburb Pacaembu, is a more original paradigm of a rationalist building (Figure 6.2). Once more an asymmetrical composition of pure volumes painted white but built with traditional masonry and featuring a still unaccomplished use of concrete, the building hosted the exhibition *The Modernist House* curated by Warchavchik during March and April 1930. The event attracted the most important Brazilian artists and intellectuals of the time, such as the poets Oswald de Andrade[20] and Mário de Andrade, the painter Tarsila do Amaral and the architect/novelist Flávio de Carvalho.[21] The exhibition acquired in the history of the modern in Brazil almost equal importance to the *Semana de Arte Moderna* that was organised in São Paulo in 1922 and marked the starting point of the Brazilian avant-garde. It was also these early works of Warchavchik that impressed Le Corbusier during his first trip to São Paulo, and he consequently invited Warchavchik to participate in the CIAM as representative of Latin America.

The fact that Warchavchik already used tropical plants and cacti in the garden of his house is an indication of an intention to adapt the European purist dogmas to the native Brazilian context, somewhat foreshadowing some of his later work, such as the residential building in Rua Barão de Limeira, São Paulo, in 1939 (Figure 6.3), or the pavilion of the Marjore Prado House, built in the province of São Paulo in 1939. The intense interplay between light and shadow in the façade of the

Rua Barão de Limeira residential building is accentuated by the building's dark ceramic base contrasting the light-coloured walls of the upper floors. The plan is organised by a tripartite division, manifested in the building's façade in the curves of the northeastern balconies. In the Marjore Prado House, Warchavchik blends the pavilion with local expressions of anonymous architecture, using very simple material means – thatched roof, bricks, wooden stakes – as well as irregular forms, to fuse the interior with the natural setting.

FIGURE 6.2 Gregori Warchavchik, Modernist House, Rua Itápolis, Pacaembu, São Paulo, 1930.

FIGURE 6.3 Gregori Warchavchik, Mina Klabin residential building, Rua Barão de Limeira, São Paulo, 1939; the building was restored in 2013 by the architect's grandson, architect Carlos Warchavchik.

Warchavchik's curved balconies came after the tenuous forms of the stairs, ramps, canopies and pool of the Brazilian Pavilion at the New York World´s Fair, in 1938–9. Designed by Lúcio Costa, Oscar Niemeyer and Roberto Burle Marx, the Brazilian Pavilion created an international sensation with the organic blending of its exterior and interior spaces and libertine horizontal planes. It also signalled the genesis of a new strand of the modern, the 'Brazilian modernism' as mentioned in contemporary historiography to differentiate it from 'modern architecture in Brazil', an umbrella under which one would classify early works such as Warchavchik's projects.[22] The Brazilian modern would reconcile, through its flowing forms and controlled voluptuousness, best represented by Roberto Burle Marx's gardens, the rationality, material and technical potential of the New Architecture with the versatility and explosive nature of the tropical climate.

Warchavchik took part in 28-year-old Lúcio Costa's attempt, in 1930, to reform the art and architectural curriculum of the National School of Fine Arts (ENBA) according to Le Corbusier's ideas and the Bauhaus values. Costa's appointment lasted only several months. He was forced to step down by the circles of the conservative tutors of the ENBA, who remained faithful to the school's French neoclassical principles. However, the support he gained from the school's students on this occasion illustrated the change of atmosphere towards the new style that would become dominant in the following decade.

In fact, two graduates of the ENBA in the 1930s, the brothers Marcelo and Milton Roberto, were the authors of another building often mentioned as the first large-scale modern building in Brazil, the Brazilian Press Association, built in Rio de Janeiro, in 1936–8. The instigator of the project was Herbert Moses, the president of the Association, who had acted as the interpreter of Frank Lloyd Wright's speeches in Rio de Janeiro in 1931.[23] The building established in Brazil the use of the concrete brise-soleil and it was the fruit of a competition organised by the Press Association in 1936. The Vargas government was maintaining a delicate balance in competitions for state commissions between the progressive and conservative tendencies that coexisted during this period in the artistic scene of the country, and this building represented the progressive. The Ministry of Education and Public Health (MESP) commission (*see* pages 81–2) is another example of the progressive.

A few days before Warchavchik's manifesto, Brazilian Rino Levi sent a letter from Rome to the São Paulo state newspaper, advocating the reinvigoration of Brazilian architecture. Levi, who was a student of architecture at the time, was equally influential in the development of the Brazilian modern. His house, built in 1944–6 and since demolished, was an example of a localised expression of modernity, with its interior courtyards and the brise-soleil insulating the various rooms towards the gardens (another work by Roberto Burle Marx). Levi's Sedes Sapientiae Educational Institute (São Paulo, 1940–42), with its characteristic screening of the main façade, is another pioneering work. It heralded, through its use of reinforced concrete and Levi's 'sophisticated preoccupation with the urban context',[24] architectural features linked with the post-war, brutalist Paulista school, of which an émigré of the mid-1940s, the Italian-originated Lina Bo Bardi, would become the most well-known representative.[25]

HOME COUNTRIES 'BY CHOICE'

One work of Bo Bardi's worth mentioning from this first period of the modern in Brazil, prior to her famous Museum of Art in São Paulo (MASP, 1957–68), is her Glass House, which she started to build for herself and her husband a few years after arriving in Brazil.[26] It was completed in 1951, the year of her naturalisation as a Brazilian. Bo Bardi's Glass House is certainly a happy moment for the *pilotis*, which fulfils its role admirably in this instance, by smoothly landing the house onto the terrain's slope and allowing the natural setting to organically 'slip' underneath, while enabling the extended glazing of the main part of the house above. Nature continues to grow without disturbance in the interior patio, where a solitary tree makes the patio reminiscent of Le Corbusier's Curutchet House, in Buenos Aires (*see* pages 33–4), with its specially planted poplar tree in the middle.[27] The way Bo Bardi's house integrates the environment is particularly significant because of the location of the vast plot in the then-remote Morumbi neighbourhood of São Paulo, among the remnants of the Mata Atlantica, the original rainforest surrounding the city.[28] It indicates Bo Bardi's affinity with the Brazilian landscape and culture. This feature of her work allowed her to further contribute to a locally developed architectural language that gained international attention, especially through the social role that her buildings assumed in the urban landscape (for example, her SESC Pompeia cultural centre, São Paulo, 1977).

Bo Bardi's house is also reminiscent of an upper-middle-class typology that can be found in Gio Ponti's work of the 1950s. Primary and secondary functions of the house are completely separated, with a wing in the northern part of the plan assigned to the servants, which turns its back to the narrow interior courtyard from which the family's rooms take light from the other side, and which is treated as a block of solid and void parts, directly touching the ground. One innovative feature in Bo Bardi's layout is the kitchen, which partially connects the two distinct areas of the residence. However, the kitchen space turns a blind wall to the courtyard, and eventually feels rather like a misfit section of the house, with its opaque walls contrasting with the airiness of the living room. Equally interesting is the choice of the shallow, double-pitched roof that uniformly covers the almost square-shaped plan of the entire house, also close to Ponti's configuration of roofs in his Venezuelan projects of the villas Planchard (1955) and Arreaza (1956).

However, not all emigrants were equally able to adapt to the new environment of their host country, despite apparent affinities. In Brazil, Bernard Rudofsky is one such example. Rudofsky is mostly known for his contribution to the 'rediscovery' of indigenous architecture and anonymous settlements of various parts of the world, thanks to an exhibition he curated at the Museum of Modern Art in New York under the title *Architecture Without Architects* (1964). Rudofsky had worked with Ponti during the mid-1930s in editing *Domus* and designing the Hotel San Michele on the island of Capri, a project that remained unbuilt. A lover of the Mediterranean culture and climate, he had published several pieces in *Domus* advocating the beneficial effects of what he called 'open-air rooms' (the concept of a patio surrounded by four walls, without a roof).

Austrian-born, he arrived in Brazil in 1938, having originally set course for Argentina. After trying Rio de Janeiro, where he was unable to integrate into architectural circles and ensure commissions, he established himself in São Paulo, where his architectural production remained limited, as it was during his whole career. An avid supporter of a 'healthy' lifestyle that even denounced the use of clothes as harmful for the human body (in the 1945 MoMA exhibition *Are Clothes Modern?*), he had difficulty establishing professional synergies. The João Arnstein House that he designed in São Paulo in 1941, which was included in the *Brazil Builds* exhibition, is a large residence made of clear geometric prisms and flat roofs, which are characteristically organised around five separate patios. Almost every room of the house thus features its own outside area, inherently blended with the inside. Rudofsky created spaces that open completely to the house's luscious, tropical gardens. The soft boundaries of these, such as wooden trellises that are covered with vegetation, borrow features from the local vernacular. Despite this example of a fine marriage between abstract aesthetics and Brazilian influences, Rudofsky was again on the move, in less than four years. In New York, he eventually had a successful career as an editor, curator, tutor and architectural critic.

The case of Hannes Meyer in Mexico draws parallels with Rudofsky. Meyer, Swiss-born and educated as a mason, tried several countries after fleeing Germany in 1930, without succeeding in finding his home country 'by choice' as Bo Bardi had.[29] Meyer was director of the Bauhaus during 1928–30; his design approach was determined by his political views. He focused on the need for low-cost infrastructure and housing and believed that architecture had little to do with aesthetics, being mainly dependent on the functional diagram of the spaces it is called to create. He emigrated first to the USSR to teach and work and although his arrival in Mexico seemed to be based on solid relations woven with the Mexican Communist Party, in the ten years he remained in the country he managed to build very few schemes. Oddly enough, considering his commitment to the social agenda of the modern, most of his work in Mexico was produced for German or Swiss émigrés of the private sector.

Meyer first visited Mexico in 1938, on the occasion of the XVI Congreso Internacional de Planificación y Vivienda (International Congress of Planning and Housing) in Mexico City, in which he participated as a lecturer.[30] He was then invited by the progressive government of Lázaro Cárdenas to collaborate with the architects Enrique Yáñez and José Luis Cuevas in the recently founded Escuela Superior de Ingeniería y Arquitectura (ESIA) (part of the National Polytechnic Institute, IPN), where they were setting up a programme of studies in urban design and planning.

Up to the first decade of the 20th century, Mexico was practically a dictatorship (under Porfirio Díaz, 1876–1911); during this period, eclecticism was the dominant style. As was similarly the case in Brazil, post-revolutionary regimes focused on the provision of housing, education and public infrastructure in general, which were considered a crucial part of the consolidation of the newly established state. Thus, the attempt of Mexican architects to define a 'national identity' was a direct result of a socio-political context, which needed to differentiate itself from the anachronistic tactics of the overthrown status quo.[31] The modern 'offered Latin American governments the means to appear modern in a variety of senses. Most obviously, it implied a modernizing economy.'[32] Mexico was a clear example of such practices, with its programmes of schools, hospitals and housing construction carried out during the first half of the 20th century. In this context, functionalist architecture was being vindicated as serving the most needed sectors of society.

Cárdenas' socialist government and its progressive reforms were well known outside Mexico and Meyer saw an opportunity to apply his ideas. He arrived in Mexico in mid-1939 and by the end of the year, together with Yáñez and Cuevas, had submitted a project for a School for Higher Studies in Planning and Urban Design. However, their proposals were systematically rejected. Emigrants relied on support from people with similar backgrounds and ideals, but in Meyer's case his political views were the reason his schemes would not be implemented. Juan O'Gorman (*see* page 71), despite being one of the first architects to promote infrastructure construction in the country with his schemes for low-cost schools (Figure 6.4), was a relentless Trotskyist. He successfully boycotted the plans of Meyer, who kept a close relationship with the USSR delegation in Mexico.[33] Cárdenas' government was not re-elected, and Meyer's ambitious plans were abandoned.

Subsequently and up to 1946, he worked for other state agencies, concentrating on the problem of social housing and on technical requirements for hospital design.[34] His most significant project was Lomas de Becerra (1942), intended for 12,500 inhabitants and including housing units of various types, as well as schools, markets, health and recreation facilities. There were also green spaces for the neighbours to socialise and to promote a healthy lifestyle.[35] It was designed for

Santa Fe, in Mexico City, and also as a prototype for future developments, but was never built.

The most relevant project Meyer realised for the private sector was the Corpus Christi block (1945), for the headquarters of a bank in the centre of Mexico City, on land previously occupied by a convent and where a chapel remained. Meyer carried out a thoughtful analysis of the site and proposed six alternatives: in some of them the chapel was removed, in some versions it was relocated, and in some it was kept at its original site.[36] Again, the project was never built but it was indicative of

FIGURE 6.4 Juan O'Gorman, primary school, Colonia Pro-Hogar, Mexico City, 1932.

the fact that Meyer's position had somewhat changed from the strict functionalist approach of his Bauhaus years. He was now exploring regionalist features, instead of the International Style architecture that people expected of him.[37] Meyer was associated with the Swiss magazine *ABC: Beiträge zum Bauen* (1924–8), which was strongly opposed to De Stijl and advocated for the absolute of science and technology in the service of the people's collective needs.[38] In Mexico he worked for the Taller de Gráfica Popular, an artistic production workshop with strong political attachments. But Meyer's disillusionment both with Russia and Mexico probably also had to do with the fact that his ideals for the supremacy of technology and technique could not easily be applied in those contexts where construction was still to a large extent based on manual work and improvisations on site. He went back to Switzerland in 1949. Despite all his efforts and his direct involvement in all aspects of welfare linked with modern architecture in post-revolutionary Mexico, Meyer's work was overlooked for decades and only began to be revisited in the 1980s.

CONTINENTAL AIRS

It is perhaps not an accident that an architect of Mexican origin was a lot more successful than Meyer in the implementation of modern ideals in the country's social housing provision. The son of a diplomat, Mario Pani Darqui (1911–83) spent the first part of his life in different cities around Europe. He graduated from the École des Beaux Arts in Paris, in 1934, and returned that same year to Mexico, where modern architecture was slowly breaking through (O'Gorman's first houses and schools, and José Villagrán García's first public hospitals, had just been built). During his first years back in Mexico, he built mostly private houses and buildings (the first ones commissioned by his uncle, who was a prominent politician and civil engineer).[39] The most noticeable building from this period is the Reforma Hotel (finished in 1936), one of the first big, modern hotels in Mexico City in the Art Deco style. Pani worked as an advisor for the first national programme of school construction, but what really made him a visionary was his awareness of the rapid growth and densification of Mexico City, which led to a serious housing shortage.

During his time as student in Paris, Pani had the opportunity to attend some of Le Corbusier's lectures, and he became acquainted first-hand with his urban theories about the Ville Radieuse.[40] In 1947, he was commissioned to design a project of 200 single houses in Mexico City; instead, he proposed a project for more than 1,000 families, which he argued was achievable on the same cost. The Presidente Alemán urban centre (Figure 6.5) was built between 1947 and 1949 and demonstrates a clear relationship with Le Corbusier's Unités d'Habitation. It consists of six 13-storey towers arranged in a zig-zag formation across the plot of land and six three-storey blocks; in all of them, the concrete and brickwork has been left exposed. There are three different types of apartment, one of which spreads over two floors with an interior staircase thus reducing the surface required for communal access. The project includes communal services (schools, shops, recreation areas, etc.) which are distributed across the scheme. All buildings are connected through pedestrian circulations, while vehicles are restricted to the perimeter. Featuring mural paintings by José Clemente Orozco, it was the first housing project of this type, and the beginning of multifamily state housing in Mexico.

In 1952, Pani completed the Centro Urbano Presidente Juárez (Mexico City), which, much like the Presidente Alemán, included communal services and spaces, and restricted the circulation of vehicles. However, the project's density was much lower and the ensemble is generally acknowledged to be more welcoming and of a more 'human' scale.[41] Here there was a greater variety of accommodation, including 12 different types of apartment, arranged in buildings of varying height, and even some single houses. In this case, some walls were decorated with low relief sculptures by the painter Carlos Mérida. The bigger Place Unité that Pani got to design was Nonoalco-Tlatelolco, built in the 1960s in Mexico City, an authentic autonomous 'city within the city' consisting of 102 towers of up to 22 storeys, originally intended for 100,000 inhabitants of different social strata.[42] It is the largest multifamily complex in the country and one of the largest in Latin America. Other significant urban planning works by Pani include the master plan for the Ciudad Universitaria, the main campus in Mexico City of the Universidad Nacional Autónoma de México (in collaboration with the architect Enrique del Moral), as part of which he also designed the Torre de Rectoría (Rector's tower). He acted as a consultant for the master plans of various cities around the country (some of which were only partially implemented).

FIGURE 6.5 Mario Pani Darqui, Centro Urbano Presidente Alemán, Mexico City, 1947–49.

For Pani the urban context was a crucial design factor, and in his Secretariat of Hydraulic Resources (1946–50, Mexico City, in collaboration with Enrique del Moral) the subtle curves speak of a sensitive integration to the site. He was also interested in exploring diversified expressions of the modern in conjunction with the place's characteristics. His Acapulco Yacht Club (1956; Figure 6.6) is a piece of architecture originating in building types of the mainstream European modern of the interwar period (*see also* Chapter 7), moulded with building techniques and materials typical of the geographical context: its round, thatched roof complements the curved horizontal planes of the building's terraces in concrete, overhanging the sea. Seen in conjunction with his design for the Acapulco airport, these two works are strongly reminiscent of the liberal geometric forms that were marking contemporary works of the Brazilian modern.

Worth mentioning also is Pani's role in promoting the acceptance of the modern in Mexico as the editor of the magazine *Arquitectura*. Founded in 1938, the magazine was originally intended to disseminate modern European architecture in Mexico. In fact, Pani would not publish any review on Mexican architecture until 1944, and then it was only about a programme of hospital construction in which he himself was taking part. Eventually, the name of the magazine changed to *Arquitectura/ México* (1946) and it began, indeed, to showcase the work of Mexican architects. Latin American architecture was reviewed for the first time in 1952, on the occasion of the VIII Congreso Panamericano de Arquitectos that took place in Mexico that same year.[43] *Arquitectura* was published for 40 years and is still considered a very valuable source for the history of Mexican architecture.

Pani's Acapulco projects are close to the regionalist strand of the modern that can be read, much earlier, in the work of a German émigré in Mexico, the architect Max Cetto (1903–80). Cetto had studied in Darmstadt, Munich and Berlin (with Hans Poelzig), worked as a state architect in Frankfurt (1926–30) and was a founder-member of the CIAM (1928) before moving to the United States in 1938 and working with Richard Neutra for a short period of time there.[44] For him, the usual itinerary of immigration (for many the USA was the final destination of their journey) was reversed. He moved to Mexico in 1940 and was naturalised in 1947. Cetto was immediately welcomed by local architects, such as José Villagrán García,

FIGURE 6.6 Mario Pani Darqui, Acapulco Yacht Club, 1956.

Luis Barragán and Juan O'Gorman. Much like Mathias Goeritz, Cetto worked with Barragán until 1955 on several projects, most importantly the Pedregal housing development.

Perhaps the most significant for his localised approach is the house that Cetto built for himself and his family in the Pedregal housing development, Mexico City

THE MODERN DIASPORA: LATIN AMERICA

(*see* pages 99–100), in stark contrast with the demonstration houses he designed with Barragán for the same site and which responded closely to an international, formal expression of the modern. In exchange for working on two demonstration houses for the scheme, Cetto received a plot of land on which he gradually built his house (the ground floor in 1949, with an upper floor added in 1952). Featuring load-bearing walls made with the local lava stone, the house is demonstrative of a mitigated version of the modern that marries the abstract prisms of the mainstream geometry and the treatment of the angle (somewhat reminiscent of Neutra's Kahn House in San Francisco, the design of which Cetto took part in) with the dominant, rough texture and sinuous forms of the land's unique natural setting.

The Quintana Weekend House that Cetto built for the Quintana family in Tequesquitengo, Morelos, in 1940, recalls the expressiveness seen in the work of his master, Hans Poelzig.[45] With its spiral staircase and rounded angles, the house (Figure 6.7) is a more emphatic effort to respond to the particularities of the site, as well as to local construction methods, of which Cetto seemed to be particularly aware:

> *In Mexico houses cannot be built by a complete set of drawings and specifications, as in most European cities and in the United States. If the architect cares to see the building finished according to his concepts, he has to supervise the work every day, playing the part of a general contractor himself. … Under such circumstances it seems considerably wiser to renounce certain ideals of mechanical perfection which we adored in the first years of functional architecture, and accept the blessings of a rather rustic, handmade and more human touch, which is probably the most adequate expression of the natural and spiritual resources of this country.*[46]

Cetto taught at the Universidad Nacional Autónoma de México, in Mexico City, from 1965 to 1979, as well as in North American universities. In 1961, he published his book *Moderne Architektur in Mexico*,[47] which presented a synthesis of his work.

FIGURE 6.7 Max Cetto, Quintana Weekend House, Tequesquitengo, Morelos, Mexico, 1940.

CONCLUSION

In Latin America the spreading of the modern was dependent both on the contribution of architects who were acquainted first-hand with its European sources and on the local architects who had their eyes turned to the mainstream.

But for those who did leave a mark on the architecture of the region, the empathy that they could demonstrate with the host country's special characteristics, as in the case of Cetto in Mexico or of Warchavchik and Bo Bardi in Brazil, was the driving force behind expressions of the modern that would distance the projects from mimetic, purely formal transpositions of concepts and would start rooting them solidly in the local context.

In Brazil, such localised expressions of modernity had given way to 'Brazilian modernism', which is internationally recognised as unique, through its irregular forms and exuberant geometry that fittingly adapts, especially when it comes to open and semi-open spaces, to the lavishness of the natural settings. In Mexico, the conditions of the construction market and cultural factors led to the adoption of decoration and typical local materials, such as the lava rubble of the Pedregal housing development, that equally set apart the Mexican modern from the polished, white cubes of the mainstream European modern of the 1920s. They provided fertile grounds for the rough aesthetics mainly of post-World War II construction, of which multifamily housing projects, such as the Centro Urbano Presidente Alemán, are characteristic. The coarse qualities of this type of building became recognisable in the construction of satellite cities in many Latin American countries and in complex stories of more recent examples, such as the spontaneous, vertical community of Torre David in downtown Caracas, Venezuela, attention to which was drawn through the studies of the Urban Think-Tank.

Both in Brazil and in Mexico, unique historical circumstances and the quest for a 'national identity' have been an important incentive for the dissemination of the modern and its exploration in ways a-typical to the hegemonic centres (i.e. France, Germany, Holland, etc.). This was less the case in the UK, where faith in local traditions and in an already well-established system of cultural values delayed the spreading of the modern and, subsequently, localised 'adaptations' of it. Nevertheless, construction techniques and materials such as apparent brickwork, closely connected with the extended timeline of British architecture, would still be at the forefront of experimentations for new 'readings' of a streamlined modernity. Questions about the ways in which the aesthetic 'prescriptions' for flat roofs or for extended glazed surfaces in the façade could be transformed and appropriated within relatively resilient geographical and cultural contexts would remain in the heart of investigations for alternative interpretations of the modern.

CHAPTER 7

MODERN DIASPORA AND THE BRITISH INTERWAR PERIOD

Apart from Latin America, there was another significant case in the history of the modern where the transplant of Continental modern architects, together with Le Corbusier's proposals in urban planning, had a considerable impact on adopting, and eventually rejecting, the New Architecture. This was the British context. Le Corbusier's influence on Britain is mostly viewed in a negative light, through post-World War II high-rise housing and social units of affordable cost associated with his Unités d'Habitation.[1] The year 2019 not only marked the centenary of the founding of the Bauhaus school, but also of the Housing, Town Planning, &c. Act 1919. This Act changed the policies of the British state regarding accommodation for those most in need, by announcing the construction of 500,000 subsidised housing units. The housing types that should predominate, and the ways subsidies should be managed by local authorities, remain subjects of debate to this day.

A prolific number and broad range of publications (both in the specialist and non-specialist press) have appeared in the British media since the interwar period revealing the story of Le Corbusier's influence, from the first translation of *Vers Une Architecture* in English, back in 1927, and of *Urbanisme* in 1929.[2] The modern in Britain is closely connected with the foundation of the Modern Architectural Research Group (MARS Group), the British branch of CIAM, by architects such as Maxwell Fry, himself closely connected to Le Corbusier (Fry and his wife Jane Drew worked with Le Corbusier in Chandigarh during the 1950s). Characteristically enough, because of a relative reluctance of British architects to adhere to the new style, MARS only came into existence in 1933, after the fourth CIAM had already taken place in Athens.

This chapter discusses architectural trends and developments in Britain during the interwar period, which has been crucial for the dissemination of the modern. It also tackles the impact of the European avant-garde that emigrated to the UK during the interwar period, driven away by changing social and financial conditions on the Continent. The concepts of the avant-garde and the developments in architecture on the other side of the Channel were discussed in the 1920s and 1930s in Britain, mainly by young talents such as Wells Coates[3] and by 'foreigners' who, even if eventually naturalised, such as Serge Chermayeff or Ernö Goldfinger,[4] still disturbed the conservative nature of the architectural profession in the country with their progressive, left-wing ideas. Continental architects who fled to the UK at the end of the 1920s and the beginning of 1930s mainly comprised Jewish Russians, and German and Austrians. These people were not well received in Britain, not least because of the saturated professional market, within which permits to work were already selectively issued to architects of considerable prestige.

THE SEEDS OF THE MODERN

The situation started to change at the outset of World War II, when it eventually became evident that there was one common enemy for all. By then, the attitudes of British society towards the modern had also altered, although preference for iconic, white, abstract volumes indicated the lag between Britain and Continental trends. More importantly, emigration seemed to have changed the game for British architecture internationally. Although only a single project had been included in the *International Style* exhibition of 1932 at the Museum of Modern Art in New York (Joseph Emberton's 1931 Royal Corinthian Yacht Club, in Burnham-on-Crouch), only five years later an exhibition was being organised at the MoMA entitled *Modern Architecture in England*. Henry-Russell Hitchcock went as far as to proclaim that England led 'the world in modern architectural activity'.[5]

One of the ways in which British architects had difficulty in adopting the principles of the modern was that these were associated with conditions of social turmoil on the Continent, which were perceived as a threat to a much-valued stability in this traditionally conservative country. Despite the need for sanitising a big part of the existing housing stock and a rising dissatisfaction during World War I among the middle and working classes about the lack of affordable units, which was partly responsible for the Housing Act of 1919 passing in Parliament, this was never actually experienced as a social uprising, as, for example, in countries of the Continent. Another aspect was difficulty in associating the modern with what was considered typically British, in terms of both morphological characteristics (such as pitched roofs) and of moral values.[6] For example, the Arts and Crafts movement celebrated the uniqueness of the product, resulting from the quality of handmade work and the intricacy of the manufacturer's craftmanship; these ideas directly contrasted with concepts of the Continental avant-garde for mass production and prefabrication in housing construction (as a tool for controlling the building costs).

Nevertheless, the modern challenged many preconceived ideas of the British architectural status quo of the interwar era, including the intellectual superiority of scholarship in architectural matters and the social role of the profession. Le Corbusier's texts were accessible to a broader public and reviewed in the non-specialist press, with their ideas of a modern life based on the positive effects of machines and devoted to the wellbeing of ordinary people. Alan Powers compared Le Corbusier's effect to that of A.W.N. Pugin's: 'Like Pugin, Le Corbusier introduced intellectuals to architectural texts, a process that was extended to other Modern Movement authors.'[7] The well-organised status of the architectural profession as a traditional guild to the service mostly of aristocratic patrons could not facilitate the dissemination of the modern. These circumstances, however, began to change in the first three decades of the 20th century, not least with the increased role that the state started assuming in housing construction.

There were signs of this change also in the way architecture was made public. The British Broadcasting Corporation (BBC) played an instrumental role in highlighting the new issues the architectural profession was called to address during the interwar period and covered a broad range of voices from different backgrounds that all brought architectural topics close to the ordinary social experience.[8] The German-born art historian Nikolaus Pevsner was an example of this change: his *Englishness of the English Art*, part of the BBC Reith Lectures he gave in 1951, came out as a book in 1956 and attempted to engage the British public in an interrogation of national identity, through artistic developments and achievements.[9]

CHAMPIONS OF THE NEW AESTHETICS

Pevsner can be credited with further acquainting the British public with the ways of the New Architecture through his *Pioneers of the Modern Movement*,[10] which he published in 1936, three years after fleeing Germany. In the middle of the century, Pevsner was still filling in gaps in scholarship, writing about Britain's building stock in its various regions, through his collaboration with Penguin Books. A series of comprehensive guides under the title *Buildings of England* started to be published in 1951 as the fruit of this collaboration. By now an established art historian in Britain, Pevsner continued to express dissatisfaction with his fellow British historians, deploring a lack of intellectual rigour among them.[11]

Pevsner was continuing, in a way, work that had been done on the subject by Hermann Muthesius; his three-volume report on the English country house,[12] published in 1904–5, provided a comprehensive review of domestic building types in Britain and offered important documentation on the work of the Arts and Crafts movement and the English Free School, which constituted a historical moment of international importance in the course of British architecture.[13] Muthesius was instrumental in the setting up of the Deutscher Werkbund, which gave birth to the Bauhaus, and was at the centre of an original exchange between Britain and Germany, conveying his interpretation of the Morrisian artistic values to a growing German middle class. Dying in a car accident in 1927, he never really adhered to the modern, making little distinction between the early designs of the Bauhaus and the superficial historicism of the 19th century, about which he was critical. Nevertheless, his ideas about an architecture fit for function and appropriate for the new cultural landscape of the industrialised era were again pushed in Britain through Bauhaus masters who escaped the Nazi regime in the 1930s.

Yet British architects did not owe their acquaintance with the modern principally to the Continental diaspora. Already in the 1920s there were British architects, such as Howard Robertson, who were reporting on the Continental developments through their journal articles.[14] F.R.S. Yorke's book *The Modern House* was published in 1934,[15] and then ran to several editions, helping to introduce modern movement architecture to a British audience; articles that he edited in *Specification* during the 1930s also made the public aware of emerging architectural ideals. Robertson's relative sympathy to the modern was also important for the instruction of the young generation of architects coming out of the Architectural Association at the end of the 1920s and the beginning of the 1930s.[16]

Le Corbusier's books were passed around students who found inspiration in the social content and technical mastery of his projects, but provoked scepticism among the older generation, who saw disturbing qualities in the new aesthetics. It was at the invitation of the students of the Architectural Association that he first visited Britain for a lecture he gave there in 1947 (interpreted by Clive Entwistle).[17] Nevertheless, his influence, at least during the interwar period, was somewhat 'virtual', as already noted for some of the countries of Latin America (*see* Chapter 6).

Except for the Venesta Plywood Company exhibition stand that he designed, together with Charlotte Perriand, for the 1930 *Buildings Trades Exhibition* in London, Le Corbusier never actually built anything in Britain.

There is an account of another project that he designed in collaboration with Clive Entwistle, an autodidact of whom little information was known until recently.[18] Entwistle also translated into English some of Le Corbusier's texts after World War II.[19] The weekend cottage (Figure 7.1) in which they worked together was built for the *Ideal Home Exhibition*, which took place at London Olympia in 1939. It is interesting as much for its layout as for its construction details. It is organised in an L-form around what is described as an 'enclosed garden', a protected courtyard which could also be heated by the living-room fireplace.[20] Reinforced concrete was used for the roof, which was planted, and reinforced brickwork for the walls was left apparent in selected parts of the house's interior. Thus, the importance of this project lies in an attempt to 'adapt' to the local construction techniques and aesthetics, which is mostly present in Le Corbusier's work after World War II. In the description of the design, emphasis is placed on the way the walls are

FIGURE 7.1 Clive Entwistle, in collaboration with Le Corbusier, weekend cottage for the *Ideal Home Exhibition*, 1939.

RETHINKING MODERNITY

articulated with the horizontal slab of the roof, so each element manifests itself as an independent part of the construction, fitting not only modern architectural standards, but also Georgian tradition.

THE AVANT-GARDE IN BRITAIN

The Venesta Plywood Company exhibition stand was commissioned by Jack Pritchard, a man who became a catalyst for several of Britain's first modern-style buildings. Pritchard, the marketing manager of Venesta, had visited the *International Decorative Arts Exhibition* in Paris in 1925, was impressed with Le Corbusier's designs and approached him through Charlotte Perriand. In 1932, together with Coates, he formed Isokon Ltd, a company inspired by the ideals of Russian constructivism. By commissioning furniture designs from several Bauhaus masters, among whom were Walter Gropius and Marcel Breuer, Pritchard offered hospitality to the Continental avant-garde both figuratively and literally. Jack and his wife Molly were the instigators of the iconic Isokon Building (Lawn Road flats, Belsize Park, Hampstead, 1932–4; Figure 7.2), which was the first real building commission of Wells Coates. The Isokon studio flats hosted émigrés such as Gropius and Breuer, László Moholy-Nagy and Arthur Korn, but also became an important meeting place for the Pritchards' broad social circle and some of the most significant British artists and writers of the period, such as Maxwell Fry, Agatha Christie and Robert Furneaux Jordan.

As a Cambridge graduate, Pritchard was associated with the broad circle of artists and designers frequenting Mansfield Forbes' house Finella, in Cambridge. He was thus able to secure the commission of the Impington Village College (Figure 7.3), New Road, Impington, Cambridgeshire, for Walter Gropius and Maxwell Fry. The partnership between Fry and Gropius, for the short period of three years that Gropius remained in Britain until he emigrated to the USA, was the result of the difficulties the émigrés faced in entering the profession.[21] According to RIBA accounts, immigrants could practise only as partners of British licensed architects or if they could establish themselves as independent practitioners with their own list of clients, which was not an easy thing to do. Immigrants were also hindered from practising as architectural assistants, although exemptions seemed to be possible.

FIGURE 7.2 Wells Coates, Isokon Building (under construction), Hampstead, London, 1932–34.

FIGURE 7.3 Walter Gropius and Maxwell Fry, Impington Village College, Impington, Cambridgeshire, 1936–39.

Impington Village College (1936–9; the school was completed after Gropius' move to the USA) was built in brick and glass and featured a series of bay windows on the northwestern side of the longitudinal wing destined for adult educational and recreational facilities. However, its asymmetric composition of varying-height volumes, and the trapezium-shaped main hall can be seen in Gropius' previous work, such as his 1929 competition design for a school in Hagen.[22] The large glazed surfaces of the classrooms faced southeast and a large part of them could open entirely to the outside, in line with modern ideals for hygienic spaces, espoused on both sides of the Atlantic. Richard Neutra had expressed such views in his 1935 article 'New Elementary Schools for America',[23] suggesting that each classroom be allowed an outdoor area of equal surface, accessible by sliding glass doors and protected by roof overhangs. In Gropius and Fry's school in Impington, the slight recess of the classrooms' glazed surfaces in relation to the brick walls and the roof structure is probably an additional effort, as well as the bay windows, to answer to local conditions, abandoning the flush lines of the avant-garde.

The Richmond Girls' High School (Figure 7.4) was designed by Denis Clarke Hall for a competition organised in 1937 by the *News Chronicle* newspaper and was built before World War II. It is another case where the architect blends modern aesthetics with traditional materials in the hope of a better integration and

FIGURE 7.4 Denis Clark Hall, Richmond Girls' High School, Yorkshire, 1937.

acceptance of the design in its local context. The project features innovations in matters of school building in the British context, such as the classrooms receiving daylight from two sides, the colour of the walls that were left white (instead of the popular chocolate brown or dark green that had been used up until this moment) and the colour of the blackboards (pale primrose yellow with a deep royal blue chalk instead of the traditional black with the white chalk). Clarke Hall had worked with Entwistle and had been influenced by him during their 'wonderful discussions about architecture'.[24] Nevertheless, the construction here was carried out with stone, while reinforced concrete was used only for secondary elements, such as portal frames, infill panels, the chimney and the main entrance canopy. It was perhaps the architect's most successful design, although Clarke Hall went on to build numerous other educational buildings after Richmond Girls' High School, which was a commission at the beginning of his professional career, secured by participating in the competition, the only one he ever entered. Furniture designed by Alvar Aalto was used for the staff room at Richmond High, and Clarke Hall designed the rest of the building's furniture.

Marcel Breuer built few projects in Britain, while working for the practice of F.R.S. Yorke, in the short period of two years (1935–7) that he spent in the country before moving to the USA, at the invitation of Gropius. Hungarian-born Breuer studied in Vienna, Austria and then Germany, at the Bauhaus, before becoming head of the school's furniture workshop. The Gane exhibition pavilion (Figure 7.5) that he designed together with Yorke for the Royal Show in Aston Court, Bristol (1936; subsequently dismantled) is in contrast with the architectural language of the Macnabb House (1936), again built in collaboration with Yorke. The Gane exhibition pavilion is interesting as an example of a 'localised' modern, such as the one featured by Richmond High, as it equally demonstrated a variety of construction materials: large glazed areas married with Cotswold stone for the walls, wood painted white for the roof structure and plywood for the interior walls, floor and ceiling. It also boasted considerably freer layout forms, while the roof sits on the supporting walls quite independently from their layout. This work is the result of an effort to produce a 'regional' version of modern aesthetics and demonstrates Breuer's conviction that new materials were not necessarily needed for modern architecture.[25]

FIGURE 7.5 Marcel Breuer and F.R.S. Yorke, Gane exhibition pavilion, Bristol, 1936.

Marcel Breuer and F.R.S. Yorke's Macnabb House ('Sea Lane House'; Figure 7.6) in East Preston, West Sussex, although somewhat moving away from earlier, more austere formal expressions by way of the sinuous curves of the living-room terrace, answers to a rather rigid layout.[26] It illustrates, in a way, both the potential and the shortcomings of the *pilotis* as a design feature. The house comprises of two wings with a clear distinction of functions; the two-storey part in the back of the plot comprises services and the kitchen on the ground floor, while the main sitting and dining areas are organised on the upper floor to take advantage of the best views.

FIGURE 7.6 Marcel Breuer and F.R.S. Yorke, Macnabb House ('Sea Lane House'), East Preston, West Sussex, 1936.

The bedroom section runs perpendicularly to the communal part of the house on the same level, supported by columns that ensure a continuation of the garden on the ground floor, which would otherwise have been divided in small, left-over parts on either side of the building. As a mixed construction of load-bearing brick walls and reinforced concrete for the bedroom wing, painted entirely in white, the house became an iconic version of an abstract modernity, fit for the seaside of the south of England. Still, the masonry walls of the Sea Lane House did not have any plaster applied to them, in order to preserve the texture of the popular, traditional material.[27] The bedroom wing, with its narrow ribbon skylight that runs only in part of the circulation space towards the communal area, offers, from the main living, interior and exterior area, a rather lame view; at the same time these main living spaces fail to establish a connection with the green space on the ground, thus foretelling the green space's disuse (it became parking for residents). This work is a lot less successful than other iconic examples of the same period that present similar configurations and rounded forms that seek to respond to the context, such as Antonio Vilar's house in San Isidro (Buenos Aires, 1937; Figure 7.7).

INTEGRATING THE MODERN

Yorke and Breuer's Sea Lane House was an example of a renewed interest in single-family houses that sprang up in Britain in the 1930s, after two decades of relatively modest construction in this domain. It reflects the change of attitude

FIGURE 7.7 Antonio Vilar, architect's house, San Isidro, Buenos Aires, 1937.

among the public and a developed taste for the clarity of the whitewashed, abstract volumes of the international modern. Two single-family houses, built by two other émigrés for their own use, are representative of a simultaneous tendency, at least among the architects that had abandoned their home countries, of responding to the new contexts with a revisited idiom of modernity. The first one, by Serge Chermayeff, was built outside London, while Ernö Goldfinger's Willow Road residence is located in Hampstead, an area of London marked by a high percentage of immigrants.

Chermayeff was also one of those who frequented the 'Finella' circle (*see* page 143).[28] The house that Chermayeff built in Sussex for his family was a subtly adapted, localised version of modernity, mainly due to the use of wood as its structural material (Figure 7.8). Strangely enough, it was the construction material that was raised by the local council as one of the main reasons for initially rejecting the scheme. Another reason was the flat roof, which was considered not to be fitting the climate of the English countryside. In any case, the debate between Chermayeff and the local council reflected the mixed feelings of British society towards the 'alien' ways of the Continent, both from an aesthetic and a cultural point of view, even in the case of an architect who had spent his early educational years in England.[29] Chermayeff was able to demonstrate the relevance of both the material and the house's flat roof volume in the architectural tradition of Sussex and its Regency-style buildings and the house was completed in 1938. It was only inhabited by the architect for a few months before he had to sell it, due to financial needs, and move to America, where he became Director of the Institute of Design in Chicago, after László Moholy-Nagy's death in 1946. It featured large sliding glass doors that almost entirely open the main living space of the ground floor to the garden and built-in furniture, designed to a large degree by the architect himself.

In the case of Hungarian-born Goldfinger, integration into British society came through his marriage with the English Ursula Blackwell. But Goldfinger was also a man of cosmopolitan airs and considerable confidence, due mainly to his connections with major artistic figures of the Continent. He established himself in London in 1934. Although having reached out to Le Corbusier during the days of his architectural studies,[30] he declared himself opposed to a 'kasbah' type of modern.[31]

FIGURE 7.8 Serge Chermayeff, the architect's house, Bentley Wood, Halland, East Sussex, 1938.

The three houses that he completed in 1939 at Willow Road were faced with bricks and significantly different from the aestheticism of the mainstream. Goldfinger was also committed to the question of science and prefabrication, which was evident in his designs for nurseries and holiday and evacuation camps and culminated in his post-war projects, of which the most representative and recognisable is the Trellick Tower in London (1967).

As well as being targeted at Le Corbusier, Goldfinger's remarks on the 'kasbah' type of modern were most probably also aimed at a fellow émigré, Berthold Lubetkin, with whom Goldfinger had had a difficult relationship, since their years of study on the Continent. The ability of Lubetkin to secure commissions and establish a reputation within the UK was perhaps another reason for this bitterness. Admittedly, Lubetkin arrived in England relatively early, in 1931, in time for the construction boom around the middle of the 1930s. Besides that, the Tecton partnership, with him as a leading member, was formed in 1932 and mostly consisted of British architects, six recent graduates of the Architectural Association, whose average age was under 30, and who decided to circumvent the internship at architectural offices, the standard way of launching an architectural career.[32]

Perhaps the most important work produced by them was the buildings of London Zoo, the most well-known being the Penguin Pool, which is now disused, having been replaced by another facility. The pool was important in demonstrating the extent of possibilities in the production of abstract forms that concrete was able to generate. The elegance and sophistication of the penguin ramps remains a unique case of an organic relationship between the material and the adopted form. Tecton's Highpoint One apartment block in Highgate, London (1935; Figure 7.9) materialised a lot of Le Corbusier's ideas about the 'vertical garden city',[33] along with modern ideals about hygienic living, integrated communal services, sports facilities and gardens, which reflected the group's commitment to architecture's social role. The building's layout, in the form of a Cross of Loraine, ensured double-aspect daylight and cross ventilation for the flats. The building gained international attention for the British modern; strangely enough, or perhaps not strangely at all, Pullman Court, designed by Frederick Gibberd during the same period, hardly had the same effect, although it had also clearly been influenced by Le Corbusier.[34]

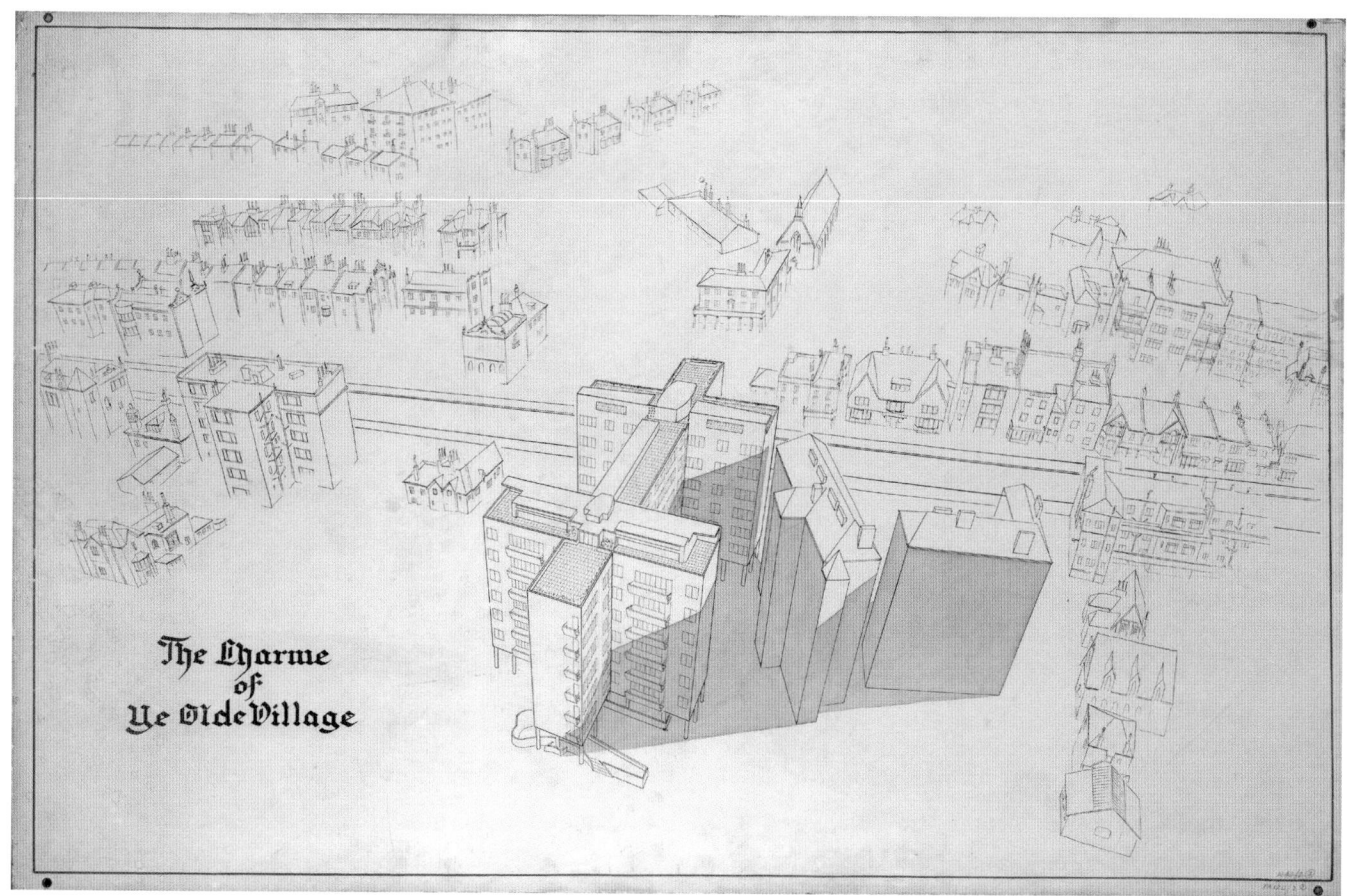

FIGURE 7.9 Lubetkin and Tecton, Highpoint One, Highgate, London, 1935, aerial view – project and surroundings.

Lubetkin also helped to disseminate the achievements of the British avant-garde on the other side of the Atlantic, through his article 'Modern architecture in England', published in 1937 in the *American Architect and Architecture* magazine.[35]

A VERY BRITISH MODERN

Around the same time, important public buildings started to appear that adopted the new aesthetics in a rather reserved manner. In such cases, the purified, prismatic geometry of the envelope was materialised through the typical texture of the traditional material. Brick walls created an impression of mass rather than volume. It was a latent modern, rather than a search for regional versions of modern, as in the case of Chermayeff's or Goldfinger's houses. The Shakespeare Memorial Theatre, built in Stratford-upon-Avon between 1929 and 1932 by Elisabeth Scott,[36] is one example of such a case; the Hornsey Town Hall, in Crouch End, London, built in 1935 by Reginald Uren, is another.[37] Both buildings answer to the principles of New Architecture, with their asymmetric compositions of pure geometric prisms and their functional layouts, but ultimately respond to a combination of both a monumental and traditional idiom. It is an architecture of heavy volumes, rendered in brick, and influenced by early examples of Swedish modernity, such as Ragnar Östberg's Stockholm City Hall (1923) or Erik Gunnar Asplund's Stockholm Library (1928), or even Marinus Dudok's design for the Hilversum Town Hall (Hilversum, the Netherlands, 1928–31). The Shakespeare Memorial Theatre (Figure 7.10) is equally characterised by its Art Deco interiors.[38] Mostly a style that was adopting the aesthetics of the modern without its social meaning and thus leaning without guilt to decorative features, and often inspired by the past, Art Deco offered an attenuated version of the modern that found solid grounds in Sweden as well as in conservative Britain.

In the interwar period, these buildings coexisted with modern masterpieces, such as the De La Warr Pavilion in Bexhill-on-Sea. Strangely enough, they were all the result of competitions. Britain has a long tradition of competitions; the first set of rules for competitions was sketched out in 1839 by an investigative committee of the newly formed Institute of British Architects. During the Victorian years, competitions were held for an impressive range of commissions: from fountains to large public buildings. This was one characteristic that set the British competition system apart from others – in the 19th century, competitions had become a regular instead of an extraordinary procedure.[39] Although, in the history of the modern movement, competitions are often considered as lost opportunities for the predomination of a dynamic avant-garde,[40] in Britain the competition system certainly had an impact on the construction of the first examples of both international and localised modern in the country, especially for public buildings, and eventually the acceptance of the modern. An important point was that competitions provided a chance to link a social agenda with aesthetic requirements.

In the case of the De La Warr Pavilion, in Bexhill-on-Sea, this social agenda was a particularly significant one for Britain's history. The real boost for seaside tourism in the UK came after World War II, but the 1920s and 1930s, despite the hard financial times, had already seen an increase in the number of people able to take a holiday for a week or so, due to rising household incomes, an improvement in workers' rights and the minimum wage, as well as in transport links. Seaside towns had to adapt to the increasing numbers of visitors, who started to represent an important commercial enterprise. They joined a race for state subsidies – the amount of money spent by each town also seemed to be an additional attraction to the holiday-makers.[41] The De La Warr Pavilion (Figure 7.11) was destined to

FIGURE 7.10 (*opposite*) Elisabeth Scott, Shakespeare Memorial Theatre, Stratford-upon-Avon, 1929–32.

FIGURE 7.11 Serge Chermayeff and Erich Mendelsohn, De La Warr Pavilion, Bexhill-on-Sea, 1935.

MODERN DIASPORA AND THE BRITISH INTERWAR PERIOD

host artistic and entertainment events and it was explicitly announced that it should be accordant with modern aesthetics, on a budget of up to £80,000. The construction of the pavilion according to the innovative design of Erich Mendelsohn and Serge Chermayeff was perhaps made possible because of a general climate that set seaside architecture apart from everyday aesthetics, allowing for an often extravagant and whimsical taste, destined to surprise and challenge. The new building would bring the sophistication of the Continent to the reach of the British working class, without the expense of a trip.

Mendelsohn arrived in Britain in 1933 as an acclaimed architect of the modern, having established a very successful practice in Germany as a designer of, among other things, large commercial buildings. Chermayeff, with whom he collaborated, before both of them moved to the USA, was already an admirer of his. They had first met during Mendelsohn's first visit to London in 1930, during an exhibition of his work at the Architectural Association. Chermayeff visited Mendelsohn, along with Jack Pritchard and Wells Coates, at his house in Berlin the following year, preparing a report about his work in the *Architectural Review*. Together, Mendelsohn and Chermayeff also had plans for a European Academy of the Mediterranean, a school adhering to Bauhaus teaching, which never came to be. Their first work together, after Mendelsohn moved to Britain, was the competition for the De La Warr Pavilion, launched the year of Mendelsohn's arrival to Britain by the mayor of Bexhill, the 9th Earl De La Warr, a person with great influence who was interested in emerging architectural trends.

The building was a construction wonder, in all its aspects. Mendelsohn came up with the design in a very short time, based partly on a cinema complex (Universum cinema) that he had completed in 1928 in Berlin.[42] Results of the De La Warr competition were announced in the *Architects' Journal*, in February 1934, and construction had already started in the first months of 1935, to be completed in the record time of 11 months. The pavilion was inaugurated in December 1935, celebrated in the local and national press as a purely contemporary building. It incorporated many innovations, being the first welded, steel-framed structure in Britain and featuring a suspended ceiling in the main hall, probably influenced by the work Chermayeff had done (together with Wells Coates and Raymond McGrath) for the interiors and cabins of the recently built Broadcasting House on Portland Place, in London (completed in 1932). Mendelsohn, in line with his mentor Frank Lloyd Wright's teachings, subtly adapted the building to the site, taking advantage of its sharp slope to the west to gain access to a basement, under the stage of the auditorium.[43] This was in line with what he had already done to ingenuously integrate the Schocken store building in one of the busy commercial streets of Stuttgart.

The large, illuminated letters spelling the building's name on the canopy, as well as the three-storey spiral staircase joining the two wings of the building together, were design devices that Mendelsohn had already used in the department stores he had created in Germany and sat well with the Art Deco style, which proved particularly popular on the seaside. The lightness of the building, especially the spacey and airy rooms of the longitudinal upper part, impresses visitors even today and speaks of the building's uniqueness, especially when compared to contemporary buildings, such as the Shakespeare Memorial Theatre.

STREAMLINED MODERN

The De La Warr Pavilion featured a streamlined modern(ism), the 'liner' or 'nautical' style, an aspect of the Art Deco (or 'jazz modern' or 'moderne') style. Liner style borrowed from naval construction in order to reflect, in the elegance of its curves, geometric decoration and shiny, metal features,[44] the cosmopolitan air and comfort of a new and exciting era (Figure 7.12).[45] The Art Deco style was not so much a separate artistic movement, as a trend which could claim kinship both with the avant-garde (in its abstract aesthetics and asymmetric volumetric arrangements, extensive glazed surfaces and preference for metal) and the traditional. In France and England, the Art Nouveau or the Arts and Crafts movement of the turn of the 20th century had established a solid footing and liner-style buildings would turn up across Europe, from Spain to Croatia (Figure 7.13), becoming icons of the modern, as identifiable as the masterpieces of the mainstream avant-garde.

A few examples of relevant buildings from other countries can provide a context for the De La Warr Pavilion and the architecture for recreational buildings of this era. In Spain, where the tradition of the Catalan modernisme of Antoni Gaudí constituted a powerful precedent for the interwar modern, the work of Luis Gutiérrez Soto

FIGURE 7.12 Eltham Palace, interior view of the mansion built in the 1930s by the Great Hall of the already existing, medieval building; a lavish residence of cosmopolitan airs.

FIGURE 7.13 Nicola Dobrović, bathing complex, Baćvice Bay, Split, competition project, 1930, view of summer restaurant.[46]

FIGURE 7.14 (*opposite*) Luis Gutiérrez Soto, Cine Barceló, Madrid, 1930.

FIGURE 7.15 Luis Gutiérrez Soto, Piscina La Isla, Madrid, 1931.

is representative of the Art Deco style. Perhaps most relevant to the De La Warr Pavilion are his Cine Barceló and the Piscina La Isla complex, both in Madrid and designed in 1930–31.[47] Cine Barceló (Figure 7.14), with its large canopy and rounded angle dominating the crossroad where it is situated, is reminiscent of Mendelsohn's expressionism of the 1920s. The new style was especially appropriate for buildings that were to serve an equally innovative programme. Similarly, in the Piscina La Isla complex (Figure 7.15), on the Manzanares river in the north part of Madrid, Gutiérrez Soto used new technologies to respond to hygiene criteria which were crucial for the building's programme of social recreation (the building, now demolished, comprised one indoor and two open-air pools). In this building, centred on a dominant central axis, the typical rounded angle is used for the central part of the main building that overlooks the largest pool. The project's dynamic, festive architecture secured it space in the pages of the magazine *AC*, edited at the time by the GATEPAC, the Spanish branch of the CIAM.

Equally, José Manuel Aizpurúa and Joaquín Labayen's Real Club Náutico in San Sebastián (1929; Figure 7.16) was hailed by the *AC* as a building of the 'new

FIGURE 7.16 José Manuel Aizpurúa and Joaquín Labayen, Real Club Náutico, San Sebastián, 1929.

generation' which has been shaped by the open-air, sun and dynamic exercise that characterise the modern lifestyle, in stark contrast with the 'sad' building of the neighbouring old Casino and its pretentious, eclectic architecture.[48] Expressive of the site's potential and offering panoramic views over the Concha Bay, it is described as a rationalist concept, the dimensions of which can usually be found only on an ocean liner. The Real Club Náutico is considered one of the first modern-style buildings of Spain, built in concrete and with a ribbon window lining almost the entire upper floor. In fact, it was to a large part built on the foundation stone walls of an aquarium previously existing on the site.

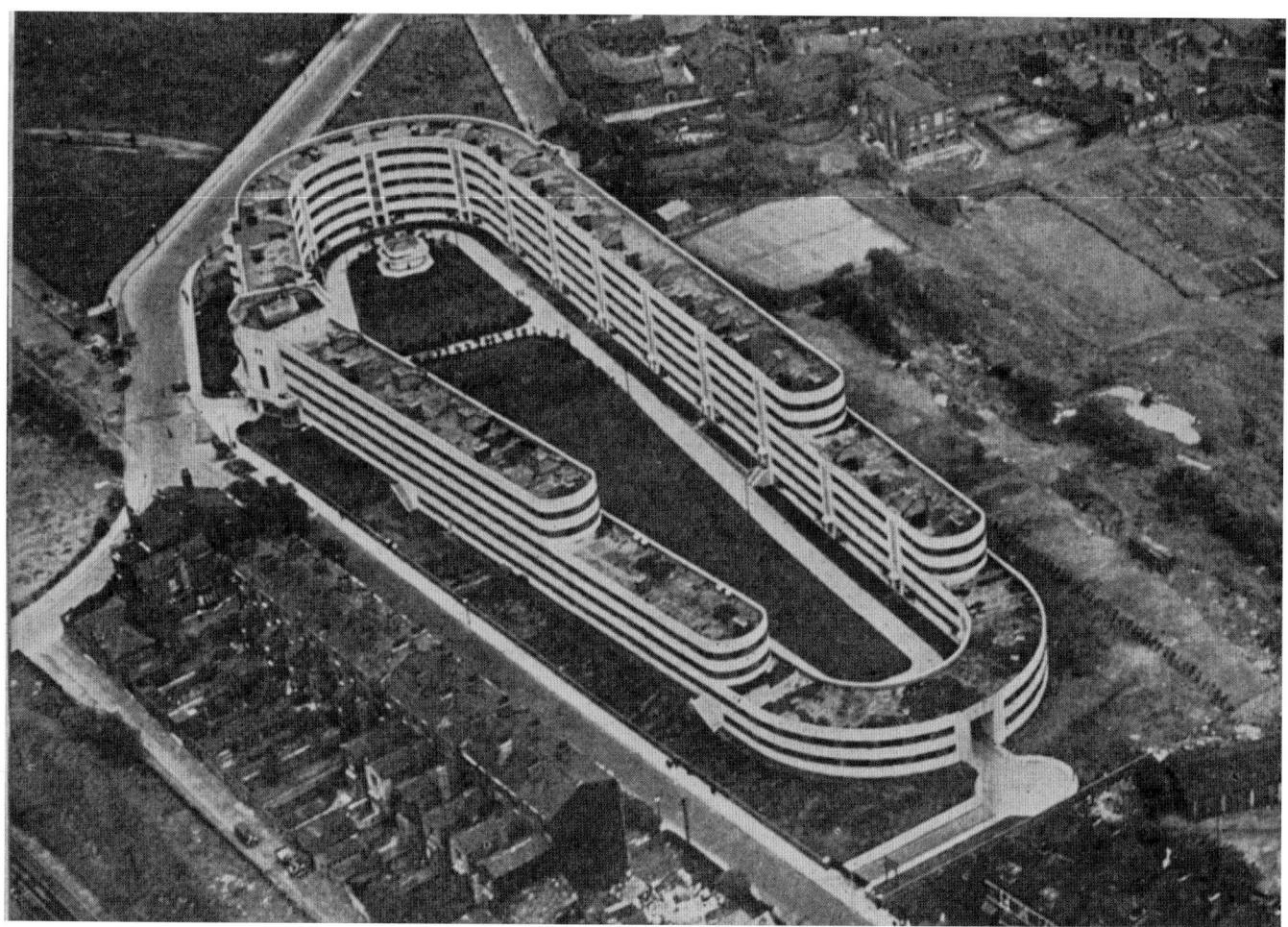

FIGURE 7.17 Richard Livett, Kennet House, Manchester, 1933–35.

In Ireland, in Sandycove, south of Dublin, Michael Scott's own house, the Geragh (1937–8), equally adopts the curved and glazed angles of the liner style. It offered panoramic views from at least two floors, including from the most important rooms of the house. Despite its proximity to the sea, the house turns its back on the beach; it initially featured a *pilotis*, which was later filled in.[49]

This kind of streamlined-modern design would be taken up in buildings of various sizes and programmes. Richard Livett's Kennet House (1933–5; Figure 7.17) is an example of a state-subsidised estate, while Peter Jones' store in Sloane Square, London (1936), by Slater and Moberly, is an instance of a commercial building which brings to mind the early work of Mendelsohn in Germany.

IN CONCLUSION

The examples listed here provide a background for the British modern, which earned international recognition thanks to buildings such as the De La Warr Pavilion, proclaimed as 'probably the most notable and successful modern building in England'.[50] This enthusiasm was due to the technical mastery that the De La Warr Pavilion featured, as well as its alternative, 'relaxed' expression of abstract geometry. This expression involved, in other projects, the return to natural materials that have always been part of the country's construction tradition and that foreshadowed a renewed interest in texture and colour that followed the end of World War II.

The diaspora had a considerable impact on the dissemination and adoption of the new aesthetics in Britain, but this only sped up a process that was already sketched out by British members of the profession. The delay in following Continental developments was in this case mainly in terms of the formal language of the modern, as technical knowledge and experimentation with industrialised processes and materials was already in place.

To summarise, concerning the two cases of Continental diaspora in Britain and Latin America, the real outburst of the modern happened in Latin America a decade later than in Britain. Traditional construction methods and conventional materials were still used in Latin America in order to achieve the desired result, well into the middle of the century. Regarding the formal expression of modernity, what happened in the countries of Latin America draws parallels with the situation in Britain, where, for the brief period between the wars, the strict formalism of the modern canon coexisted with experiments for a more 'regional' approach. However, there can be no comparison in terms of the material and technical means available in each case; similarly, there can be no doubt of the greater impact that a relatively freer-layout geometry and looser volumetric compositions have had in the definition of a typically 'national', Brazilian modern(ism).

AFTERWORD

The preceding chapters do not represent an exhaustive study of alternative modernisms. Materials, forms and, most importantly, design principles suggestive of a regional approach to modernity can be seen in examples from around the world, and are not limited to countries of the European periphery or Latin America. These examples constitute an unfailing source of study for scholars focusing on modernity and its ramifications for contemporary architecture.

In Asia, the influence of the mainstream modern has been decisive for the formulation of a relevant architectural language; the mentorship of the best-known avant-garde architects, such as Le Corbusier or Mies van der Rohe, has been crucial for Asian modernity. Among the most representative cases are Minnette de Silva (1918–98), often mentioned as Sri Lanka's first modern architect, or Chung-up Kim (1922–88), an iconic figure of the modern in South Korea.

Chung-up Kim worked at Le Corbusier's studio from 1952 to 1955, before returning to Korea to set up his own practice. Together with Jong-sung Kim (1935-), who worked at Mies van der Rohe's office for ten years (after graduating from the Illinois Institute of Technology and until 1972), and Swoo-geun Kim (1931–86), who was a student of the Japanese architect Kenzo Tange (1913–2005), all three represent the first generation of the modern in Korea, which gained ground in the country after independence from the Japanese colonial regime (1910–45) and the Korean War (1950–53). In projects such as the Pusan National University and the French Embassy in Korea, by Chung-up Kim, traditional Korean architectural elements are married with international features of the modern. In Swoo-geun Kim's work, Japanese colonial influences can be traced, along with an intense investigation for an architecture fitting for a newly founded independent Korean state that would, at the same time, make the country worthy of discussion on the international scene. Consequently, modernity in Korea is frequently connected with projects of large scale and public buildings, as is also often the case in Latin American countries.

De Silva entertained a lifelong friendship with Le Corbusier, whom she met in 1946 during a trip to Paris. De Silva participated in the sixth CIAM (hosted in Bridgwater, UK, in 1947) still as an architectural student in London. She graduated from the Architectural Association (AA) in 1948 (the same year that her country gained full independence from the UK), and upon her return to Sri Lanka became one of the very few women in the world at that time to hold their own architectural practice. She was also the first woman of Asian origin to become a RIBA associate. In her work, traditional morphologies, such as enclosed, shaded courtyards and verandas with lush vegetation, are blended with globalised abstract geometry. She was also original in her participative approach to the design of housing developments.

Most importantly, De Silva is often associated with the influential relationship between British architectural schools, such as the AA, and Asian and African modernity, through the British colonial network and what is often referred to as 'tropical' modern(ism). Her 'adapted' modern approach was developed in the educational post-war context of the AA, where the question of 'inventing' an appropriate modernity for sultry climates was becoming an integral part of reconsidering the principles of a globalised architectural style. The AA's iconic Department of Tropical Architecture was founded in 1954 (after De Silva's graduation), but De Silva had already become an inspiration for younger Asian architects, such as her compatriot Geoffrey Bawa (1919–2003), who graduated from the AA in 1957, and is more commonly mentioned among the pioneers of a climate-responsive modernity. Bawa was particularly concerned with materials that would age well in tropical conditions, an attitude typical of the 'tropical' modern that was taught at the AA by architects such as the German-born Otto Königsberger (1908–99), Jane Drew (1911–96) and Maxwell Fry (1899–1987). Königsberger had spent many years practising architecture in colonial India and advocated the reinterpretation of local building traditions instead of simply importing western technologies in tropical countries of the world. By working on various commissions for educational buildings in the decade after the end of World War II, Drew and Fry were among the architects who directly influenced the output of modernity in African countries, especially in the western part of the continent.

Similarly to what happened in parts of Asia, such as Sri Lanka and Korea, troubled social backgrounds and the struggle for independence from colonial regimes and protectorates formed a big influence on African modernity. This flourished considerably later than modernity in Europe and the Americas. In a context striving to confirm identities of independence, commissions of big public works, such as civic and educational buildings, were relatively frequent and provided a chance for 'imported' architects to work on building programmes to which it would be difficult to have access in their countries of origin. The absence of architectural schools in Africa in the first half of the 20th century meant that the few local young people who could afford it attended architectural schools in Europe. This allowed foreigners originating from countries with interests in Africa, such as Britain, France, Belgium or Italy, to act as protagonists in local architectural scenes well into the 1960s.

The French architects Fernand Pouillon (1912–86) and Henri Chomette (1921–95) practised in Africa in search of the ideal commissions, being disappointed by the status quo of the construction markets in their own country. Pouillon, who was active mainly in Algeria and remains a problematic figure in architectural history due to a tumultuous professional life, aimed to produce low-cost housing of high living quality, while paying careful attention to local social and material resources and landscapes. His architecture was innovative in the way it reinvented traditional construction logics and morphologies, and in the use of materials such as stone that diverge from what was then considered as typically 'modern'. The Bureaux d'Études Henri Chomette (BEHC) was founded after Chomette won a famous international competition for the Imperial Palace of Ethiopia (1948–51), one of the first competitions organised under the auspices of the UIA (Union Internationale des Architectes).[1] BEHC was active in 23 countries in sub-Saharan Africa during the three decades of reconstruction after World War II (known as the *Trente Glorieuses* [Glorious Thirty]). Chomette was keen to understand the local context and produce, by assimilating and reinterpreting, an architecture fit for the 'image' of the new regimes and for the needs of a young society. The result of all these often conflicting forces in African modernity is a palimpsest of styles, with local morphologies and materials blending with modern aesthetics and rules to produce unexpected outcomes.

Across the world, alternative streaks of the modern remain understudied, and viewed as anomalies. Yet architects such as Fernand Pouillon have produced work that is characterised by their unique, personal architectural vocabularies, created by exploring contexts or conceptual themes that are new to them, which they have 'adopted'. The Czech-born American Antonin Raymond (1888–1976), who was active in Japan and was a collaborator with Frank Lloyd Wright on the Imperial Hotel in Tokyo (1916), is another similar example. Even if such bodies of work are also often marked by volatility and variance, which renders in-depth study difficult, it is worth the effort as frequently these architects produce innovative interpretations and ideas.

Alternative approaches to the modern often display an intense focus on the user and the particularity of their lifestyles, which is a trait of a humane architecture where the rigid geometry of a canonical modernity, especially as broadly promoted in central Europe and North America during the interwar period, appears softened and eased. This is perhaps the result of a more intimate relationship between architects/users and their natural environments, as well as between architects and the clients. The architecture of Bawa, Luis Barragán or Dimitris Pikionis, which seems to reach the zenith of their genius when it comes to the arrangement of gardens, landscapes and exterior spaces, offers ample testimony to the first part of this hypothesis, while the example of Gio Ponti, who stressed building as a mutual learning experience for both the architect and the client, speaks of the second.

A strong point of interest in the work of alternative modern architects, especially the ones often referred to as 'critical regionalists', is the emphasis they place on intricate craftmanship. De Silva's projects display latticework, decorative tiles, balustrades and woven panels, in a bid to create a unique Sri Lankan architectural legacy of modernity. An extended technical know-how and a large experience of local materials and techniques is what can bring an added value of care and consideration, especially with building projects such as houses, which represent unique stories of everyday life and which still make up the largest part of our built environment.

Computational design and production of building components often means the dissociation of the architectural professional from the construction process, most importantly in the educational context of the young architect. In the act of building and the work of an architect, there will always be a practical expertise that can only be acquired on the construction site. Effective, innovative practices are ultimately associated with a hands-on approach to a material art, such as architecture.

AFTERWORD

Contemporary design attitudes that preach a self-evidenced predominance of technology over art and creative intuition risk eventually slighting the human being (both the designer and the users).

Much as the idea of eliminating human error from the design process seems appealing, architectural space is intended for humans and therefore can only be suitably conceived by human 'inventors.' Hardcore principles that argue for constant differentiation in forms and spatial experiences, while advocating for a contemporary avant-garde approach, risk diminishing important pieces of collective memories, and gradually removing architecture's social connection and meaning. Nevertheless, refuting the implementation of technological advancements can only mean an unrealistic perception of the present and a retrogressive interpretation of the future.

In times when the theory and history of architecture seem to play only an accessory role to design, if any at all, seen as derogative, fastidious exercises in a reality that seems to be moving on fast-track, the study of resilient, adaptable design logics offers food for thought for the moment when architectural creation again comes into perspective. Regional approaches to modernity nourished seeds for an environmentally friendly interpretation of the modern, creating an investigation thread that remains profoundly timely today. Most importantly, architects who adopted such attitudes questioned dogmas and hegemonic paradigms, and demonstrated, above all, a holistic understanding of their art, engaging in lifelong, toilsome explorations of it; they configured space as complex correlations of a multitude of factors centred around the user, privileged challenge over assertion, polyphony of views over the predominance of a specific doctrine, and eventually created a wonderful, fascinating array of possibilities.

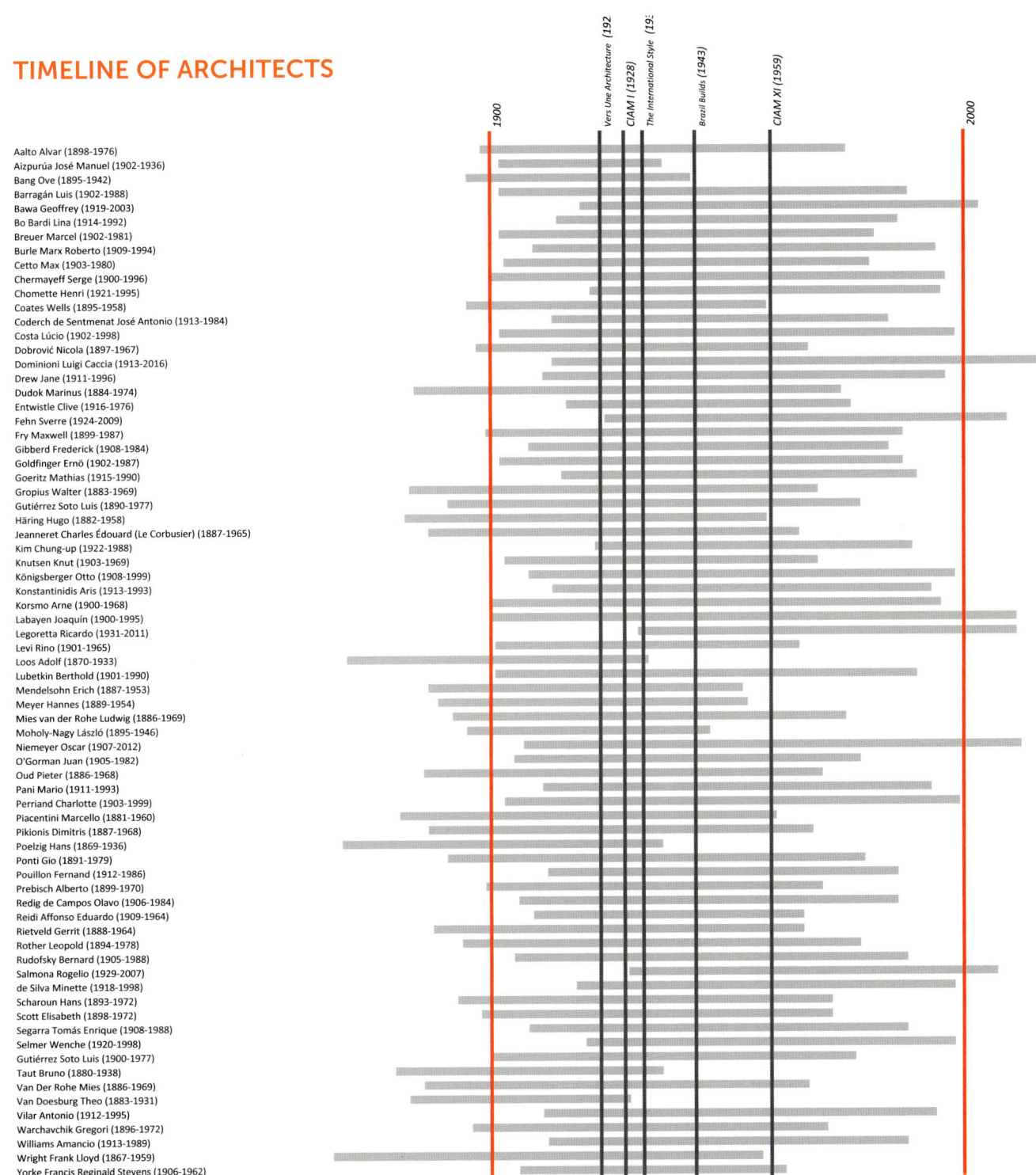

ENDNOTES

FOREWORD

1. C. St John Wilson, *The Other tradition of modern architecture: the uncompleted project*, London, Academy Editions, 1995.
2. P. Ricœur, 'Universal Civilization and National Cultures', 1961. Originally published in *History and Truth*, Evanston, IL, Northwestern University Press, 1965, pp 271–84, trans. Charles A. Kelbley. Reprinted courtesy of Northwestern University Press.
3. K. Frampton, *Modern Architecture. A Critical History*, London, Thames and Hudson, 1985, p 314.
4. A. Colquhoun, 'Form and Figure', *Oppositions* 12 (Spring 1978), 1978, p 33.
5. See D. Mertins, *Modernity Unbound: Other Histories of Architectural Modernity*, London, Architectural Association Publications, 2011, p 187.

INTRODUCTION

1. H. Heynen, *Architecture and Modernity: A Critique*, Cambridge, MA, and London, MIT Press, 1999, p 3. For the terms *modernity*, *modernisation* and *modernism*, Heynen relies upon M. Berman, *All that is Solid Melts into Air: The Experience of Modernity*, London, Verso, 1982.
2. This is better understood when one considers publications about the alternative modern, in languages other than English, German or French, by native-speakers. In such cases, the regional modern is mostly described as 'Mexican' or 'Brazilian', 'Italian' or 'Greek'; rarely is the term modernism employed and, often, it is in a negative way, enclosing the idea of an intent of *mimesis* that went wrong in execution.
3. H.-R. Hitchcock and P. Johnson, *The International Style: Architecture since 1922*, New York, W.W. Norton & Co, 1932; N. Pevsner, *Pioneers of the Modern Movement from William Morris to Walter Gropius*, London, Faber & Faber, 1936; S. Giedion, *Space, Time and Architecture: The Growth of a New Tradition*, Cambridge, MA, Harvard University Press, 1941.
4. *See* on this subject M. Crinson, *Rebuilding Babel: Modern Architecture and Internationalism*, London and New York, I.B. Tauris, 2017, especially Chapter 3, 'Well-ventilated utopias – Le Corbusier, CIAM and European modernism in the 1920s'.
5. P. Tournikiotis, *The Historiography of Modern Architecture*, Cambridge, MA, MIT Press, 1999, p 15.
6. K. Frampton, *Modern Architecture: A Critical History*, London, Thames & Hudson, 1980.
7. *See*, for example, A. Colquhoun, *Modern Architecture*, Oxford, Oxford University Press, 2002.
8. As cited in the book's third and revised edition, K. Frampton, *Modern Architecture: A Critical History*, London, Thames & Hudson, 1992, p 2. The book's second edition (1987) already concluded with a chapter on critical regionalism.
9. K. Frampton, *A Genealogy of Modern Architecture: Comparative Critical Analysis of Built Form*, Zurich, Lars Müller Publishers, 2015, p 8.
10. J.L. Bonillo and G. Monnier (eds.), *La Méditerrannée de Le Corbusier*, Aix-en-Provence, Publications de l'Université de Provence, 1991, pp 137–61.
11. *See* V. Fraser, *Building the New World: Studies in the Modern Architecture of Latin America 1930–1960*, London and New York, Verso, 2000, p 15 and note 41, p 259.
12. *See*, for example, W. Curtis, *Modern Architecture since 1900*, Oxford, Phaidon, 1982.

CHAPTER 1

1. J.M. Montaner, *La modernidad superada*, Barcelona, Gustavo Gili, 1997, cited from second edition (2016), p 25.
2. *Architecture without Architects* was the title of a book published by the Museum of Modern Art (MoMA) in New York and Bernard Rudofsky in 1964, to accompany an exhibition of the same name, and focusing on the qualities of vernacular architecture around the world. (*See also* note 11.)
3. *See* on that subject F.L. Lara, 'One step back, two steps forward: The maneuvering of Brazilian avant-garde', *Journal of Architectural Education*, vol. 55, no. 4, 2002, pp 211–18.
4. The Grande Hotel of Ouro Preto, built in Minas Gerais in 1939 by Oscar Niemeyer, is the most representative example of this

idea. For his modern design to be built, Niemeyer was convinced by Costa to introduce a ceramic-tile roof and wooden trellises to blend in with the rest of the city.

5   Ponti published this text separately in a book format several years later: G. Ponti, *La casa all'italiana*, Milan, Domus, 1933.
6   G. Ponti, *In Praise of Architecture*, New York, Dodge, 1960, p 91.
7   Casa Elettrica was in fact a collective project, in which Adalberto Libera also collaborated.
8   It is worth remembering here that Pompeii has been a source of inspiration for many modern masters. Le Corbusier visited Pompeii in October 1911 as part of his Voyage d'Orient; he talked about how architecture 'was revealed' to him through this trip. See J.F. Lejeune and M. Sabatino (eds.), *Modern Architecture and the Mediterranean: Vernacular Dialogues and Contested Identities*, New York, Routledge, 2010, pp 15–39.
9   G. Ponti, 'Una villa alla Pompeiana', *Domus*, vol. 79, pp 16–19 (author's translation from the Italian).
10 On the connection between the insular architecture of the Aegean and the modern, *see* G. Simeoforidis and G. Tzirtzilakis, 'Méditerranéité et modernité, le dernier voyage en Grèce', in *Le Corbusier et la Méditerrannée. Ouvrage réalisé à l'occasion de l'exposition Le Corbusier et la Méditerrannée, Marseille, Centre de la Vieille Charité, 27 Juin–27 Septembre 1987*, Marseille, Éditions Parenthèses, 1987, pp 63–71.
11 Rudofsky (1905–88) studied the vernacular architecture of concrete on the island of Santorini in his doctorate dissertation, which he later used, along with material he had accumulated during his extensive travels in Southern Europe, to put together the *Architecture without Architects* exhibition at the Museum of Modern Art in New York (1964) and in the accompanying publication.
12 A separate School of Architectural Engineering was not inaugurated in the National Technical University of Athens (NTUA) until 1917.
13 Aegina served briefly (1828–9) as the capital of the newborn Greek state, after the Greek War of Independence against the Turks.
14 As cited in A. Tzonis and A. Rodi, *Greece: Modern Architectures in History*, London, Reaktion, 2013, p 120. *See also* K. Vrieslander and J. Kaimi, *Rodakis' House in Aegina*, 1934, reprinted in Greek, Athens 1997.
15 D. Pikionis, Autobiographical Notes, 1958, as reprinted (translated into English) in D. Pikionis, *A Sentimental Topography*, London, Architectural Association, [c. 1989], p 37.
16 Cited in A. Pikioni and Nt. Rokou-Pikioni (eds.), *Δημήτρης Πικιώνης 1887–1968* [Dimitris Pikionis 1887–1968], Athens, Benaki Museum, p 124 (author's translation).
17 *See* C. Bouras, 'Ο Πικιώνης και οι αρχαίοι Έλληνες' ['Pikionis and the ancient Greeks'], in D. Antonakakis et al. (eds.), *Δημήτρης Πικιώνης. Αφιέρωμα στα εκατό χρόνια από τη γέννησή του* [Dimitris Pikionis: A Century from his Death], Athens, NTUA, 1989, pp 135–46.
18 D. Pikionis, Autobiographical Notes, in *Dimitris Pikionis: A Sentimental Topography*, p 37.
19 The programme remains unique in Europe for its scale and achievement, as more than 1,800 school buildings were built in the space of a few years.
20 *See* A. Ferlenga, *Pikionis 1887–1968*, Milan, Electa, 1999. Affinities with Adolf Loos' work can also be found in the arrangement of openings in the main façade of the Papaloukas residence (1927–33).
21 D. Pikionis, Autobiographical Notes, in *Dimitris Pikionis: A Sentimental Topography*, p 37.
22 *See* D. Pikionis, *Κείμενα. Δημήτρης Πικιώνης, 1887–1968* [Texts 1887–1968], Athens, Morphōtiko Hidryma Ethnikēs Trapezēs, 1986, p 73.
23 A. Ferlenga describes Pikionis as this in *Le strade di Pikionis*, 'Siracusa: Lettera Ventidue', p 9 (author's translation).
24 J.M. Buendía Júlbez, J. Palomar and G. Eguiarte, *The Life and Work of Luis Barragán*, trans. M. Brooks, New York, Rizzoli, 1997, p 10.
25 Ibid. Bac, German-born and French-educated, an amateur architect and gardener, aims at 'a renewal of the Spanish Mediterranean style', as he mentions in an inscription he makes on a copy of his illustrated story *Les Colombières*, for Barragán, when they meet.
26 Buendía Júlbez, Palomar and Eguiarte, *The Life and Work of Luis Barragán*, p 10.
27 Pikionis also launched, together with a group of friends, the short-lived journal **Το Τρίτο Μάτι** [*The Third Eye*], 1935–7, where architectural texts and translations of texts by architects such as Le Corbusier and Erich Mendelsohn were published among varied artistic topics and reviews.
28 For Pikionis, the articles of the popular art of his country stand for the same universal values that make up the spirit of the place: *see* T. Moutsopoulos, '**Ζωγραφική**' ['Painting'], *in* A. Pikioni and Nt. Rokou-Pikioni (eds.), *Δημήτρης Πικιώνης 1887–1968* [Dimitris Pikionis 1887–1968], Athens, Benaki Museum, 2010, pp 33–4.
29 As Alan Colquhoun mentions, Kiesler also made part of the circle of friends of the Dadaist film-maker Hans Richter, as did Mies van der Rohe (when resuming his practice in Berlin after World War I), van Doesburg and El Lissitzky. *See* A. Colquhoun, *Modern Architecture*, Oxford, Oxford University Press, 2002, p 172.
30 K. Frampton, *Modern Architecture: A Critical History*, London, Thames & Hudson, 1980.
31 R. Peltason and G. Ong-Yan, *Architect: The Pritzker Prize Laureates in their own Words*, London, Thames & Hudson, 2010, p 356.

CHAPTER 2

1. Interior walls and partitions need not depend any more on the structural footprint of the building. The same goes for the façades, which can now be organised independently from the segmentation of the interior space.
2. W. Gropius, 'Flach-, Mittel- oder Hochbau?' [Low, middle or high-rise building?], Lecture at the Third International Congress for New Building, Brussels, 27–9, November 1930, *Das neue Frankfurt*, January 1931, https://digi.ub.uni-heidelberg.de/diglit/neue_frankfurt1931/0037/image (accessed 15 January 2019). Published in English for the first time in 1935 in his book *New Architecture and the Bauhaus*, a year after he fled Nazi Germany, first to Britain and, eventually, the USA.
3. *See* on this subject B. Colomina, *Privacy and Publicity: Modern Architecture as Mass Media*, Cambridge, MA, and London, MIT Press, 1994. The elimination of certain architectural elements, such as the entrance pergola of Villa Schwob in La Chaux-de-Fonds, contributed to profiling the project in an uncompromised, authentic, purist manner.
4. *See also* on this subject P. Blundell Jones, 'The Photo-dependent, the photogenic and the unphotographable', in A. Higgott and T. Wray (eds.), *Camera Constructs: Photography, Architecture and the Modern City*, Surrey and Burlington, Ashgate, 2012, pp 50–51.
5. H.-R. Hitchcock and P. Johnson, *The International Style: Architecture since 1922*, New York, W.W. Norton & Co, 1932.
6. I. Ábalos, *La buena vida: Visita guiada a las casas de la modernidad*, Barcelona, Gustavo Gili, 2000, pp 13–36.
7. *See* https://farnsworthhouse.org/portfolio-items/designed-for-the-floodplain/?portfolioCats=80 (accessed 18 January 2019).
8. R128 is a four-storey house that is self-sufficient, in terms of heating energy requirements, and completely recyclable.
9. *See* on this subject A. Colquhoun, *Modern Architecture*, Oxford, Oxford University Press, 2002, p 172.
10. There has recently been an initiative for the reconstruction of the Wolf House, which was destroyed in the last days of World War II, in 1945, *see* https://www.nytimes.com/2016/04/01/arts/design/rebuilding-a-modernist-gem-from-mies-van-der-rohe.html (accessed 8 December 2018).
11. *See* http://www.fondationlecorbusier.fr/corbuweb/morpheus.aspx?sysId=13&IrisObjectId=5415&sysLanguage=en-en&itemPos=66&itemCount=78&sysParentId=64&sysParentName= (accessed 8 December 2018).
12. *See* http://www.fondationlecorbusier.fr/corbuweb/morpheus.aspx?sysId=13&IrisObjectId=5913&sysLanguage=fr-fr&itemPos=86&itemCount=215&sysParentName=Home&sysParentId=65 (accessed 14 December 2018).
13. Emilio Ambasz (b. 1943) later became curator of architecture and design for the Museum of Modern Art (MoMA) in New York (1969–76); an early proponent of 'green' architecture himself, he has helped draw international attention to Luis Barragán, curating the 1974 MoMA exhibition *The Architecture of Luis Barragán*.
14. C. Norberg-Schulz, *Modern Norwegian Architecture*, Oslo, Norwegian University Press, 1986, p 67. *See also* Chapter 3.
15. Together with Christian Norberg-Schulz, Arne Korsmo and other Norwegian architects of the same generation, as well as the Danish Jørn Utzon (with whom Korsmo maintained family friendship), Fehn formed PAGON (Progressive Architects Group Oslo Norway), which was the Norwegian branch of CIAM (International Congress of Modern Architecture), probably around 1948–50.
16. As cited by Norberg-Schulz, *Modern Norwegian Architecture*, p 97.
17. E. Tostrup, 'Norwegian Wood – Wenche Selmer style', *Nordisk Arkitekturforskning*, 2000:4, p 73.
18. Ibid, p 80.

CHAPTER 3

1. The painter Jesus (Chucho) Reyes Ferreira is one of the people Barragán thanks in his Pritzker Prize acceptance speech in 1980. *See* L. Barragán, 'Luis Barragán 1980 Laureate Acceptance Speech', 1980, p 3, Pritzker Prize website, https://www.pritzkerprize.com/sites/default/files/inline-files/1980_Acceptance_Speech.pdf, (accessed 4 July 2018). Chucho Reyes is one of the painters and artists frequenting the circle of Diego Rivera and Frida Kahlo that rekindled interest in Mexico's cultural heritage in the 1920s through their interest in traditional arts.
2. *See also* on this subject D. Pauly, *Barragán: Space and Shadow, Walls and Colour*, Basel, Boston and Berlin, Birkhäuser, 2002, pp 148–52.
3. Rivera had also acted as Barragán's adviser for the Pedregal project, see Pauly, *Barragán: Space and Shadow, Walls and Colour*, p 21.
4. The Rivera Kahlo studio house and the house that O'Gorman built for his father Cecil O'Gorman in 1929 are considered Mexico's first functionalist buildings.
5. Le Corbusier and Ozenfant signed together the manifesto of *purism* in 1921, while together with Fernard Léger they published the magazine *L'Esprit Nouveau* in the 1920s.
6. V. Fraser, *Building the New World: Studies in the Modern Architecture of Latin America 1930–1960*, London and New York, Verso, 2000, pp 44–5.
7. J.M. Buendía Júlbez, J. Palomar and G. Eguiarte, *The Life and Work of Luis Barragán*, trans. M. Brooks, New York, Rizzoli, 1997, p 71.
8. Mathias Goeritz was an architect, painter and sculptor. A German émigré, he arrived in Mexico in 1949, with an invitation from Barragán's friend, Ignacio Díaz Morales, to teach at the University of Guadalajara, where Morales was head of the architecture department at the time. He became a close friend and collaborator of Barragán.

9. As quoted in Pauly, *Barragán*, p 183.
10. Barragán did the same with other parts of the construction; occasionally, he would reduce heights, or add an extra partition wall, when construction had already advanced on site.
11. Pancho Gilardi, who together with his colleague and cofounder of an advertising firm, Martin Luque, commissioned the Gilardi House from Barragán, giving him a free rein, recalled in an interview that the architect had been reflecting on the right colour for one wall in the house's interior pool space for more than a month.
12. Barragán, 'Luis Barragán 1980 Laureate Acceptance Speech', p 2.
13. Pauly, *Barragán*, pp 151–2.
14. Ibid, pp 192–3.
15. Ibid, p 7.
16. See C. Maniaque, *Le Corbusier and the Maisons Jaoul*, New York, Princeton Architectural Press, 2009.
17. See A. Rüegg, *Polychromie Architecturale: Le Corbusier's Color Keyboards from 1931 and 1959*, Basel, Birkhauser, 1997, p 16.
18. See on this subject A. Rüegg, 'On color restoration of the Villa Savoye', trans. L. Widder, *A+U*, March 2000, Special Issue: *Visions of the Real: Modern Houses in the 20th Century*, vol. I 1900–49, pp 198–201.
19. This was the first exhibition of De Stijl in France.
20. See Rüegg, *Polychromie*, p 22.
21. Ibid, pp 94–143.
22. As mentioned in A. Ozenfant and C.-E. Jeanneret [Le Corbusier], 'Purisme', *L'Esprit Nouveau*, no. 4, 1921, and cited by Rüegg, *Polychromie*, p 43.
23. Rüegg, *Polychromie*, pp 113, 121, 127.
24. Ibid, p 19. An example is the ultramarine, ochre and grey revealed in the 1987 restoration of the Villa Schwob in La Chaux-de-Fonds (1916–17).
25. Rüegg, *Polychromie*, p 30.
26. See also B. Klinkhammer, 'The Spatial Use of Color in Early Modernism', Proceedings of the 87th ACSA Annual Meeting, Legacy and Aspirations, 1999, https://www.acsa-arch.org/chapter/the-spatial-use-of-color-in-early-modernism (accessed 23 November 2019), p 224.
27. For a full account of the project, *see* E. Tostrup, *Planetveien 12: The Korsmo House, A Scandinavian Icon*, London, Artifice Books on Architecture, 2014.
28. According to Elisabeth Tostrup, Korsmo often mentioned Dudok in his lectures and he had seen the Hilversum Town Hall on a trip in 1928 (email communication between Tostrup and the author on 4 October 2018). *See also* Tostrup, *Planetveien 12*, p 58.
29. Both Villa Stenersen and Villa Dammann were designed for well-off clients who gave the architect free rein. About Villa Stenersen, *see also* http://www.nasjonalmuseet.no/en/visit/locations/Villa+Stenersen.9UFRHQ2b.ips (accessed 30 September 2018).
30. A. Skjerven Astrid, '"Like a sculptural painting": Arne Korsmo's interior architecture in Norway after World War II', *Studies in the Decorative Arts* 6, no. 1, Fall–Winter 1998–9, pp 2–31, http://www.jstor.org/stable/40662660 (accessed 15 September 2018).
31. See C. Norberg-Schulz, *The Functionalist Arne Korsmo*, Oslo, Universitetsforlaget, 1986.
32. Mexico had also been an indirect source of inspiration after Arne and Grete's visit to the USA (1949–50), where they became friends with Charles and Ray Eames and admired their collection of colourful Mexican artefacts; see Tostrup, *Planetveien 12*, p 67.
33. The aesthetic, idealistic approach of De Stijl also strongly opposed the materialistic New Objectivity of the German-speaking modern, besides contrasting Le Corbusier's more 'architectural' strategy regarding colours.
34. See P. Blundell Jones, 'The photo-dependent, the photogenic and the unphotographable', in A. Higgott and T. Wray (eds.), *Camera Constructs: Photography, Architecture and the Modern City*, Surrey and Burlington, Ashgate, 2012, pp 59–60 (note 7).
35. Ibid, p 48.
36. Konstantinidis had been Pikionis' assistant at the National Technical University of Athens.
37. Hélène de Mandrot was the owner of the La Sarraz castle, where the fist CIAM took place in Switzerland, in June 1928.
38. The projects are mentioned by Frampton as a version of vernacular modernism; see K. Frampton, *A Genealogy of Modern Architecture: Comparative Critical Analysis of Built Form*, Zurich, Lars Müller Publishers, 2015, pp 11–12.
39. *See* T. Benton, 'The Villa de Mandrot and the place of the imagination', in M. Richard (ed.), *Massilia 2011: Annuaire d'Études Corbuséennes*, Marseille, Editions Imbernon, 2011, pp 92–105.
40. Le Corbusier, *Œuvre Complète*, vol. 2, 1929–34, as quoted at http://www.fondationlecorbusier.fr/corbuweb/morpheus.aspx?sysId=13&IrisObjectId=5415&sysLanguage=en-en&itemPos=66&itemCount=78&sysParentId=64&sysParentName= (accessed 21 September 2018).
41. D. Leatherbarrow, *Uncommon Ground*, Cambridge, MA, MIT Press, 2000, p 194.
42. For additional details, *see* A. Tzonis and A. Rodi, *Greece: Modern Architecture in History*, London, Reaktion, 2013, pp 137–8; 157–8.
43. Concrete was in fact not so new a material for the Greeks, as a kind of concrete can be found already in the vernacular constructions of the volcanic land of Santorini; equally, Greek engineers and architects contributed a lot in developing the material's performance, in its early period.
44. Labour was cheap and relatively easy to find, especially in post-war Greece. S. Philippou explains the same circumstances in the case of the free-form Brazilian modern, *see* S. Philippou, *Oscar Niemeyer: Curves of Irreverence*, New Haven, CT, and London, Yale University Press, 2008, p 101.

45 Krokos is also known for his sensitivity in colour and his painter's eye.
46 Makris has collaborated with Krokos on a number of projects. His drawings are representative of his interest in painting and colours, mainly from an architectural point of view.
47 Souvatzidis has been influenced by both Pikionis and Konstantinidis but has his own personal architectural idiom that comprises environmentally friendly construction techniques, tightly connected with an attentive use of materials and colours.
48 *See* L. Arvaniti-Krokou, E. Konstantopoulos and A. Levidis (eds.), ***Κυριάκος Κρόκος*** [Kyriakos Krokos], Athens, Benaki Museum, p 146.
49 *See* on that subject E. Beaumont, 'A wolf in sheep's clothing', *The Architectural Review*, vol. CCXLIV, issue 1454, 2018, pp 112–14. Van de Velde coats the doors 'in a thin layer of ethereal silver-leaf, reflecting soft light into the spaces' (p 112).
50 *See* R. Gregory, 'Les Graines D'Étoiles nursery by Atelier Fernandez & Serres, Aix en Provence, France', *Architectural Review*, 1 December 2009, https://www.architectural-review.com/today/les-graines-detoiles-nursery-by-atelier-fernandez-and-serres-aix-en-provence-france/5218326.article (accessed 21 September 2018).

CHAPTER 4

1 Cited from A. Loos, *Ornament and Crime*, 1908, as translated and published in B. Miller and M. Ward (eds.), *Crime and Ornament: The Arts and Popular Culture in the Shadow of Adolf Loos*, Toronto, YYZ Books, 2002, p 30.
2 Ibid, p 33.
3 Le Corbusier, *L'art décoratif d'aujourd'hui*, Paris, Editions Crès, 1925, p xxiii.
4 *See* on that subject H.-R. Hitchcock and P. Johnson, *The International Style: Architecture since 1922*, New York, W.W. Norton & Co, 1932, p 41.
5 Cited from Loos, *Ornament and Crime*, as translated and published in *Crime and Ornament: The Arts and Popular Culture in the Shadow of Adolf Loos*, p 30.
6 *See* Hitchcock and Johnson, *The International Style*, p 69.
7 P. Blundell Jones, 'The photo-dependent, the photogenic and the unphotographable', in A. Higgott and T. Wray (eds.), *Camera Constructs: Photography, Architecture and the Modern City*, Surrey and Burlington, Ashgate, 2012, p 49.
8 Ibid.
9 *See* B. Colomina, *Privacy and Publicity: Modern Architecture as Mass Media*, Cambridge, MA, and London, MIT Press, 1994, pp 264–9 (as in fifth edition of 2000).
10 *See* J. Quetglas, 'Lo placentero', *Carrer de la Ciutat*, nos. 9–10, special issue on Loos (January 1980), p 2, as cited in the fifth edition of Colomina, *Privacy and Publicity*, p 265.
11 Besides the Goldmann and Salatsch store, see also Knize Men's Outfitters (Vienna, 1910–13).
12 For a thorough analysis of Loos' approach in this seminal text, contemporary context and theoretical ramifications, see J.J. Lahuerta, *On Loos: Ornament and Crime*, trans. G. Thomson, Barcelona, Tenov, 2015.
13 Hitchcock and Johnson, *The International Style*, p 69.
14 See D. Pauly. *Barragán: Space and Shadow, Walls and Colour*, Basel, Boston and Berlin, Birkhäuser, 2002, p 104.
15 The overhead lighting, the cantilevered parts, the glazed north façades, the metal frames for the windows, which can be seen, for example, in the house Le Corbusier built for Amédée Ozenfant in 1923.
16 O'Gorman was appointed in 1932 (the same year he completed Kahlo and Rivera's house; *see* pages 48–9) by Minister Narciso Bassols; Bassols was seeking to reform educational architecture to represent the change of regime in the post-revolutionary Mexican society.
17 On this subject, see I. Rodriguez-Prampolini, 'Juan O'Gorman: Arquitecto y pintor', Mexico City, Universidad Nacional Autónoma de México (UNAM), 1982; I. Miranda-Zacarias, 'Standard and Non-standard: A Study of the Historical Development and Evaluation of the Present-day Performance of Primary School Architecture in Mexico', Oxford Brookes PhD thesis, 2011.
18 Rodríguez-Prampolini, *Juan O´Gorman: Arquitecto y pintor*.
19 As cited in C. Bamford Smith, *Builders in the Sun: Five Mexican Architects*, New York, Architectural Book Publishing Co., 1967, p 18.
20 As cited in Rodríguez-Prampolini, *Juan O´Gorman: Arquitecto y pintor*, p 44 (translated by the author).
21 *See* B. Brooks Pfeiffer and G. Nordland (eds.), *Frank Lloyd Wright in the Realm of Ideas*, Carbondale, Southern Illinois University Press, 1988. *See also* on this subject the analysis by Henry Russell-Hitchcock in MoMA, *Modern Architecture: International Exhibition, New York, February 10 to March 23, 1932*, New York, MoMA, 1932, pp 35–6.
22 As cited in Bamford Smith, *Builders in the Sun*, p 28.
23 Ibid, p 29.
24 *See* on this subject V. Fraser, *Building the New World: Studies in the Modern Architecture of Latin America 1930–1960*, London and New York, Verso, 2000, pp 22–4.
25 Ibid, p 75.
26 *See* Bamford Smith, *Builders in the Sun*, pp 9–10.
27 This is especially true in the example of Juan O'Gorman's Rivera Kahlo House.
28 Bamford Smith, *Builders in the Sun*, p.14.
29 *See* S. Philippou, *Oscar Niemeyer: Curves of Irreverence*, New Haven, CT, and London, Yale University Press, 2008, p 101.
30 Ibid, p 73.

31 See https://blogdoims.com.br/casa-walther-moreira-salles-por-guilherme-wisnik (accessed 15 September 2018).
32 See L. Carranza and F. Luiz Lara, *Modern Architecture in Latin America: Art, Technology and Utopia*, Austin, University of Texas Press, 2014, pp 108–12. The landscape design of the project was done by Roberto Burle Marx. The building is today known as the Palácio Gustavo Capanema, named after the minister who commissioned it.
33 The design was by Arquímedes Memoria, who succeeded Lúcio Costa as director of the Escola Nacional de Belas Artes (ENBA: National School of Fine Arts).
34 Le Corbusier repeatedly included the building in exhibitions of his own work without mentioning the Brazilian team; this caused Costa's intervention for the correction of facts. For the evolution of the design, *see* Philippou, *Oscar Niemeyer*, p 58.
35 The Ministry was completed during World War II, in 1945. Capanema had also solicited foreign artists for this artwork: Marc Chagall, Fernand Léger and André Masson. See http://euroacademia.eu/wordpress/wp-content/uploads/2015/06/Patricia_Freitas_Modernity_and_Identity_in_S%C3%A3o_Paulo_During_the_1950%E2%80%99s_-_Three_Murals_from_C%C3%A2ndido_Portinari.pdf> (accessed 18 September 2018).
36 See MoMA, *Portinari of Brazil*, New York, Museum of Modern Art, 1940, pp 8–9, https://www.moma.org/documents/moma_catalogue_2987_300190164.pdf (accessed 18 September 2018).
37 D. Ghirardo, *Italy: Modern Architectures in History*, London, Reaktion, 2013, p 107.
38 M. Romanelli, *Gio Ponti: A World*, Milan, Abitare Segesta in association with the Design Museum, 2002, pp 74–5.
39 Ibid, p 74.
40 A green-coloured marble with white veins, its name was derived from the characteristic layering of the material being similar to an onion.
41 See Gio Ponti Archives online, http://www.gioponti.org/en/archives/work-detail/dd_32990_6060/italian-culture-institute-lerici-foundation (accessed 15 July 2018).
42 Romanelli, *Gio Ponti: A World*, pp 124–7.

CHAPTER 5

1 B. Brooks Pfeifer (ed.), *Frank Lloyd Wright Collected Writings, Volume 1*, New York, Rizzoli, 1992, pp 100–01.
2 B. Brooks Pfeifer (ed.), *Frank Lloyd Wright Collected Writings, Volume 5*, New York, Rizzoli, 1995, p 216.
3 B. Zevi, *Towards an Organic Architecture*, London, Faber & Faber, 1950 (first published 1945).
4 A. Colquhoun, *Modern Architecture*, Oxford, Oxford University Press, 2002, p 202.
5 J. Pallasmaa, 'Villa Mairea – Fusion of Utopia and Tradition', published at https://www.villamairea.fi/en/villa-mairea/#arkkitehtuuri (accessed 20 October 2018), as an abridgement of the original article published in Y. Futagawa (ed.), *GA: Alvar Aalto: Villa Mairea, Noormarku, Finland, 1937–1939*, Tokyo, A.D.A. Edita, 1985.
6 On this subject and the connection between Wright and Cubism *see* M. Engel, 'Frank Lloyd Wright and Cubism: A study in ambiguity', *American Quarterly*, vol. 19, no. 1, 1967, pp 24–38.
7 See J. Lucan, *Composition, non-composition: Architecture et théories, XIXe–XXe siècles*, Lausanne, Presses Polytechniques et Universitaires Romandes, 2009, pp 343–4.
8 See H-R. Hitchcock, 'Frank Lloyd Wright', in MoMA, *Modern Architecture. International Exhibition, New York, February 10 to March 23, 1932, Museum of Modern Art*, New York, MoMA, 1932, p 32.
9 See V. Scully, Jr., *Modern Architecture: The Architecture of Democracy*, New York, George Braziller; London, Prentice-Hall, 1961, p 21.
10 F.L. Wright, *A Testament*, New York, Horizon Press, 1957, pp 323–34.
11 Le Corbusier, *Œuvre complète, 1910–1929*, 1929, vol. 1.
12 E. Frank, *Pensiero organico e architettura Wrightiana*, Bari, Dedalo Libri, 1978, p 32. (Author's translation into English of the original: 'Al simbolo corbusieriano dell'uomo col braccio alzato, che occupa spazio, Wright contrappone l'uomo in movimento che fende lo spazio. Con Le Corbusier l'accento è sulla verticale, sull'uomo e l'architettura che sfidano la gravità; con Wright, invece, è sull'orizzonte, sullo spazio e l'uomo fluenti e mobili sulla superficie terrestre.')
13 See N. Levine, 'Frank Lloyd Wright's diagonal planning revisited', in R. McCarter (ed.), *On and By Frank Lloyd Wright: A Primer of Architectural Principles*, London and New York, Phaidon, 2005, pp 232–63.
14 Wright and Aalto also shared a deep interest in traditional Japanese architecture that is evident for Aalto in the case of the Villa Mairea project.
15 See Zevi, *Towards an Organic Architecture*, p 56.
16 Ibid, p 75. Zevi notes: 'The biological or anthropomorphic fallacy is at the root of expressionism. It gave rise to the conviction that houses should represent sentiments, states of mind or the actual content of the building, it was in fact a phenomenon of decadence.'
17 By the theoretician Adolf Behne; *see* Colquhoun, *Modern Architecture*, pp 99, 169–70.
18 'The expressionists ... tried to express the content of a building symbolically through an exuberant, arbitrary plasticism within a literary and mystico-romantic atmosphere.' Zevi, *Towards an Organic Architecture*, p 31.
19 P. Blundell Jones, 'The photo-dependent, the photogenic and the unphotographable', in A. Higgott and T. Wray (eds.), *Camera Constructs: Photography, Architecture and the Modern City*, Surrey and Burlington, Ashgate, 2012, p 53.
20 As cited in F. Irace, *Gio Ponti: La casa all'italiana*, Milan, Electa, 1988, p 151. (Author's translation into English of the

original: '*Non dobbiamo mai chiudere le prospettive, dobbiamo far vedere "più che si può", far infilate, fughe, aperture di luci.*').

21. R. De Cáceres, 'El confort espacial como argumento del diseño de la vivienda colectiva', *Quaderns d'arquitectura i urbanisme*, 256, 2007, pp 149 (author's translation into English of the original in Spanish: Con Gio Ponti, las diagonales ya no son fruto de la geometría de la planta, sino que nacen de la voluntad de diluir el espacio, de convertirlo en una escenografía cambiante.).

22. *See*, for example, L. Spinelli, *José Antonio Coderch: La cellula e la luce*, Rome, Testo & Immagine, 2003, as part of the series *Universale di architettura*, initiated by Bruno Zevi.

23. For more details on his work *see* F. Irace and P. Marini (eds.), *Luigi Caccia Dominioni: Case e cose da abitare; stile di Caccia*, Venice, Marsilio, 2001 (illustrated with photos by Gabriele Basilico).

CHAPTER 6

1. H.-R. Hitchcock, *Latin American Architecture since 1945*, New York, MoMA, 1955. *See also* V. Fraser, *Building the New World: Studies in the Modern Architecture of Latin America 1930–1960*, London and New York, Verso, 2000, pp 3–4.
2. Le Corbusier used to attack the academic status quo, and always declined any involvement in academic teaching. *See* C. Braun and J. Cacciatore (eds.), *Arquitectos Europeos y Buenos Aires 1860–1940*, Buenos Aires, Fundación TIAU, 1996, pp 115–24.
3. Ibid, pp 103–14. A member of GATEPAC (the Spanish branch of CIAM, founded in 1930 by, among others, Josep Lluís Sert and José Manuel Aizpurúa), Bonet emigrated to Argentina, initially setting up practice with Kurchan and Ferrari Hardoy, the famous Grupo Austral.
4. F. Luiz Lara, 'One step back, two steps forward: The maneuvering of Brazilian avant-garde', *Journal of Architectural Education*, vol. 55, no. 4, 2002, pp 211–18.
5. Prebisch is the architect who designed in 1936 one of the landmarks of Buenos Aires, the obelisk commemorating the city's foundation.
6. J.F. Liernur, *Arquitectura en la Argentina del siglo XX: La construcción de la modernidad*, Buenos Aires, Fondo Nacional de las Artes, 2001, pp 171–3; T. Béchini, 'Construire Buenos Aires, 1880–1960', *Bulletin de l'Institut Pierre Renouvin*, no. 37, 2013, pp 29–42, https://www.cairn.info/revue-bulletin-de-l-institut-pierre-renouvin1-2013-1-page-29.htm (accessed 15 January 2018).
7. A. Sartoris, *Gli elementi dell'architettura funzionale*, Milan, Hoepli, 1932. This was one of the first efforts to gather the most prominent examples of modern architecture internationally. The book was published the same year as *The International Style* and featured a prologue by Le Corbusier.
8. This is mentioned in A. Humanes, 'Memoria de ausentes', *Revista Arquitectura*, no. 314, 1998, pp 100–1, http://www.coam.org/media/Default%20Files/fundacion/biblioteca/revista-arquitectura-100/1993-2000/docs/revista-articulos/revista-arquitectura-1998-n314-pag100-101.pdf (accessed 15 January 2018).
9. Albers visited various Latin American countries more than a dozen times in the period between 1935 and the late 1960s. An exhibition entitled *Josef Albers in Mexico*, with his work and collages from this period, was held at the Solomon Guggenheim Museum, New York, in 2017–18; *see* https://www.guggenheim.org/artwork/artist/josef-albers (accessed 15 January 2018).
10. The monument was to be erected with the cooperation of all governments and peoples of the Americas but was not completed until 1992, more than two decades after the death of the architect who won the competition and designed the scheme, the Scottish architect Joseph Lea Gleave.
11. *See* A. Irigoyen, 'Frank Lloyd Wright in Brazil', *The Journal of Architecture*, vol. 5, issue 2, 2010, pp 135–7.
12. Others included the Venezuelan Augusto Tabito Acevedo (1953–9) and the Chilean Guillermo Jullian de la Fuente (1958–65).
13. The house has since been demolished. *See* on this subject I. Wouters et al. (eds.), *Building Knowledge: Constructing Histories* (vols 1 & 2), 6th International Congress on Construction History (Brussels, Belgium), Leiden, the Netherlands, CRC Press/Balkema, 2018.
14. Today this building is home to the Museum of Architecture Leopoldo Rother; *see* http://www.facartes.unal.edu.co/museo-arquitectura/edificio.html (accessed 31 January 2018).
15. The author is especially grateful to the Colombian architect Jorge Anibal Manrique Prieto for drawing her attention to Rother and Violi's cases, as well as for all valuable information provided about Colombian modernity, see <http://www.architecthum.edu.mx/Architecthumtemp/paisajesarquno/Manrique.htm>. *See also* M. Quantrill, *Latin American Architecture: Six Voices*, College Station, Texas A&M University Press, 2000, and especially in the same work 'Introduction', by M. Waisman, pp 3–19.
16. *See* I. del Cueto Ruiz-Funes, 'México', in C. Burkhalter et al. (eds.), *Arquitecturas desplazadas: Arquitecturas del exilio Español*, Spain, Ministerio de Asuntos Exteriores, 2010.
17. *See* I. Miranda-Zacarias, 'La Arquitectura de Enrique Segarra Tomás en la ciudad de Veracruz', *in* I. San Martin Córdova and F. Winfield Reyes (eds.), *Miradas desde adentro y hacia afuera: Interpretaciones regionales y nacionales de Movimiento Moderno*, Mexico, DOCOMOMO-México/Universidad Veracruzana, 2015, pp 47–64.
18. Eureka got the contracts for all public buildings and infrastructure in the programme of modernisation of Veracruz.

See A. Vázquez, *La construcción de los sueños: Vida de Manuel Suárez y Suárez*, Mexico, Fondo Documental Manuel Suárez, 2012.

19. L. Cavalcanti, *When Brazil was Modern: A Guide to Architecture 1928–1960*, trans. J. Tolman, New York, Princeton Architectural Press, 2003, pp 350–53.
20. Oswald de Andrade was the author of the *Manifesto antropófago* [Cannibalistic Manifesto].
21. *See* Cavalcanti, *When Brazil was Modern*, p 354. Many of these artists later worked alongside Lúcio Costa for the Serviço do Patrimônio Histórico e Artístico (SPHAN), created by the Ministry of Education in 1937 with the aim of rediscovering the country's heritage, cultural richness and identity.
22. Luiz Lara, 'One step back, two steps forward,' p 212.
23. *See* Cavalcanti, *When Brazil was Modern*, p 299.
24. L. Carranza and F. Luiz Lara, *Modern Architecture in Latin America: Art, Technology and Utopia*, Austin, University of Texas Press, 2014, p 219.
25. Before emigrating to Brazil, Lina Bo Bardi had collaborated in Milan with Carlo Pagani in practice, with Gio Ponti in the magazines *Lo Stile* and *Domus*, and with Bruno Zevi in setting up the weekly magazine *A – Attualità, Abitazione, Arte*.
26. Bo Bardi was involved with Italy's Communist Party during World War II, which made it difficult for her to secure commissions in the still-conservative, post-war Italy.
27. Curiously, the poplar corresponds to the 'Mussolini' type, originating from Italy. *See* https://casacurutchet.net/2013/11/14/le-corbusier-casa-curutchet (accessed 15 December 2018).
28. *See* 'Glass House/Lina Bo Bardi', *ArchEyes*, 15 August 15 2016, http://archeyes.com/glass-house-lina-bo-bardi (accessed 15 January 2019).
29. This is how Bo Bardi described Brazil.
30. P. Rivadeneyra, 'Hannes Meyer en México (1938–1949)', *in* INBA, *Apuntes para la historia y la crítica de la arquitectura Mexicana del siglo XX: 1900–1980*, vol. 1, Mexico, INBA, 1982, pp 115–40.
31. I. Miranda-Zacarias, 'Standard and non-standard: A study of the historical development and evaluation of the present-day performance of primary school architecture in Mexico', PhD thesis, Oxford Brookes University, 2011.
32. Fraser, *Building the New World*, p 7.
33. Rivadeneyra, 'Hannes Meyer en México'. A. Toca Fernández, 'Héroes y Herejes: Juan O'Gorman y Hannes Meyer', *Casa del Tiempo*, no. 32, June 2010, pp 18–23.
34. A. Mendez-Vigata, 'Política y lenguaje arquitectónico: Los regímenes posrevolucionarios en México y su influencia en la arquitectura pública, 1920–1952', *in* E. Burien (ed.), *Modernidad y Arquitectura en México*, Mexico, GG, 1997, pp 61–90.
35. R. Franklin Unkind, 'Experiencias de urbanismo: Los proyectos urbanos de Hannes Meyer en México (1938–1949)', *Dearq*, no. 12, July 2013, pp 28–41.
36. Ibid.
37. *See also* Carranza and Lara, *Modern Architecture in Latin America*, p 102.
38. *See* A. Colquhoun, *Modern Architecture*, Oxford, Oxford University Press, 2002, pp 180–81.
39. C. Bamford Smith, *Builders in the Sun: Five Mexican Architects*, New York, Architectural Book Publishing Co., 1967.
40. L. Noelle, 'La arquitectura y el urbanismo de Mario Pani: Creatividad y compromiso', *in* E. Burian (ed.), *Modernidad y arquitectura en México*, Mexico, GG, 1997, pp 179–91.
41. The Centro Urbano Presidente Juárez consisted of 984 flats for some 3,000 inhabitants, on a plot of land of 25 ha. This was far from the 1,000 inhabitants/ha in Le Corbusier's proposals, applied by Pani in the Presidente Alemán (1,080 flats in an area of 4 ha), *see Arquitectura/México*, no. 67, September 1959.
42. One of the buildings collapsed during the earthquake of 1985 and many others were severely damaged and had to be demolished. Today most of its inhabitants are of low or very low income, and many apartments have been abandoned.
43. L. Noelle, 'América Latina en las páginas de la revista Arquitectura/México', *in* I. San Martín and F. Winfield (eds.), *Miradas desde adentro y hacia afuera: Interpretaciones regionales y nacionales del Movimiento Moderno*, Mexico, DOCOMOMO-México/Universidad Veracruzana, 2015, pp 145–55.
44. *See also* about Cetto and his work in Mexico, A. Schätzke, *Transantlantische Moderne: Deutsche Architekten im lateinamerikanischen Exil*, Munich, Verlagshaus Monsenstein und Vannerdat, 2015, pp 70–81, 133–6.
45. Perhaps Poelzig's most well-known work is his expressionist masterpiece Großes Schauspielhaus, in Berlin, which he renovated in 1919 and has since been demolished.
46. Max Cetto, interview in *Arts and Architecture* 68, August 1951, as cited in W. van den Bergh (ed.), *Luis Barragán: The Eye Embodied*, Maastricht, Pale Pink Publishers, 2006, pp 4–5, https://www.researchgate.net/publication/274566360_Luis_Barragan_The_Eye_Embodied (accessed 15 January 2019).
47. M. Cetto, *Moderne Architektur in Mexico*, Stuttgart, Verlag Gerd Hatje, 1961.

CHAPTER 7

1. *See* A. Ferster Marmot, 'The legacy of Le Corbusier and high-rise housing', *Built Environment*, vol. 7, no. 2, 1981, pp 82–95.
2. *See* on that subject I. Murray and J. Osley (eds.), *Le Corbusier and Britain: An Anthology*, Abingdon and New York, Routledge, 2009.
3. Coates was himself a 'foreigner', a Canadian who came to London in 1922.
4. Goldfinger was Hungarian-born, as well as a Marxist.
5. H.-R. Hitchcock, 'Modern architecture

in England', in Museum of Modern Art, *Modern Architecture in England*, The Museum of Modern Art, New York, 1937, New York, Museum of Modern Art, 1937, p 25.

6   See R. Blomfield, 'Is Modernism on the right track?', *The Listener*, 26 July 1933, and 'For and against modern architecture', *The Listener*, 28 November 1934.

7   A. Powers, 'Introduction', in I. Murray and J. Osley (eds.), *Le Corbusier and Britain: An Anthology*, Abingdon and New York, Routledge, 2009, p 5.

8   See on this subject S. Yusaf, *Broadcasting Buildings: Architecture on the Wireless, 1927–1945*, Cambridge, MA, MIT Press, 2014.

9   N. Pevsner, *The Englishness of English Art: An expanded and annotated version of the Reith Lectures broadcast in October and November 1955*, London, Architectural Press, 1956.

10 N. Pevsner, *Pioneers of the Modern Movement from William Morris to Walter Gropius*, London, Faber & Faber, 1936.

11 See B. Cherry, 'Introduction to The Modern Movement in Britain by Nikolaus Pevsner,' in Twentieth Century Society, *British Modern Architecture and Design in the 1930s. Twentieth Century Architecture*, no. 8, London, Twentieth Century Society, 2007, p 14.

12 H. Muthesius, *Das Englische Haus: Entwicklung, Bedingugnen, Anlage, Aufbau, Einrichtung und Innenraum: in 3 Bänden*, Berlin, Wasmuth, 1904–5. For the English translation, D. Sharp (ed.), *The English House*, London, Frances Lincoln, 2007.

13 On that subject, see C. Moore, 'The English House by Hermann Muthesius, edited by Dennis Sharp, Frances Lincoln, London,' *Architectural Research Quarterly*, 13(3-4), 2009, 325–8.

14 See, for example, H. Robertson, 'Architecture of the Modernist School', *The Architect and Building News*, 19 April 1927, pp 745–8.

15 F.R.S. Yorke, *The Modern House*, London, Architectural Press, 1934.

16 See A. Powers, *Britain: Modern Architectures in History*, London, Reaktion, 2007, p 36.

17 His second visit, during which he visited again the AA, was when he received the RIBA Gold Medal, in 1953. See also 'Corb at the AA', https://www.aaschool.ac.uk/AASCHOOL/LIBRARY/Corb.pdf (accessed 15 January 2019).

18 See on that subject R. Pinkham, 'Light on Entwistle', *Architectural review*, vol. 164, no. 980, October 1978, p 204.

19 See C. Entwistle (transl.), *Concerning Town Planning* [Propos d'urbanisme], London, Architectural Press, 1946; C. Entwistle and G. Holt (transl.), *The Home of Man* [La Maison des hommes], London, Architectural Press, 1948.

20 See A. Hastings (ed.), *Week-end Houses, Cottages and Bungalows*, London, Architectural Press, 1939, pp 66–7.

21 In the USA, Gropius took the position of Director at Harvard University's Graduate School of Design.

22 See A. Schätzke, *Deutsche Architekten in Großbritannien: Planen und Bauen im Exil 1933–1945*, Stuttgart and London, Axel Menges, pp 88–91; Harvard Art Museums' collection, 'Competition entry for the Hagen Engineering School, Hagen, 1929', https://www.harvardartmuseums.org/art/165443 (accessed 15 January 2018).

23 R.J. Neutra, 'New Elementary Schools for America', *Architectural Forum*, January 1935, pp 24–35.

24 D. Clarke Hall, 'School design in the 1930s', in Twentieth Century Society, *British Modern Architecture and Design in the 1930s. Twentieth Century Architecture*, no. 8, 2007, p 71.

25 See Schätzke, *Deutsche Architekten in Großbritannien*, pp 82–3.

26 See the same publication in which the weekend cottage by Entwistle and Le Corbusier appears: Hastings, *Week-end Houses, Cottages and Bungalows*.

27 See Schätzke, *Deutsche Architekten in Großbritannien*, pp 86–7.

28 This was through his employment at the Waring and Gillow interior design company. McGrath and Forbes, who refurbished the 'Finella' in 1928, had visited Waring and Gillow, while working on the house commission.

29 A Russian, Chermayeff graduated from Harrow School in 1917 and then studied in England, Germany, Austria, the Netherlands and France. He started his career as an interior designer when back in England in 1924.

30 See N. Warburton, *Ernö Goldfinger: The Life of an Architect*, London, Spon, 2002.

31 G. Stamp, 'Conversation with Ernö Goldfinger', *Thirties Society Journal*, no. 2, 1982, p 32, as cited in R. Elwall, *Ernö Goldfinger*, London, Academy Editions, 1996, p 13.

32 See P. Coe and M. Reading, *Lubetkin and Tecton: Architecture and Social Commitment*, London, Arts Council of Great Britain; Bristol, The University of Bristol, 1981, p 69.

33 Le Corbusier, 'The Vertical Garden City', *The Architectural Review*, no. 79, 1936. The block gained praise from Le Corbusier himself when he visited, after its completion in 1935.

34 See C. Hui Lan Manley, *Frederick Gibberd*, Swindon, Historic England; London, RIBA Publishing, 2017, pp 10–13.

35 B. Lubetkin, 'Modern Architecture in England', *American Architect and Architecture*, no. 150, 1937, pp 29–42.

36 Elisabeth Scott's first architectural position was at the practice of Herbert Wigglesworth and David Niven, which had Scandinavian connections and a reputation for training young architects.

37 Uren was born in New Zealand.

38 The term Art Deco was first coined in the late 1960s, at the occasion of a retrospective exhibition at the Musée des Arts Décoratifs in Paris, as a shortened version of the 1925 *Exposition des Arts Décoratifs et Industriels Modernes*; until then, many alternative terms were used.

39 J. Bassin, *Architectural Competitions in*

Nineteenth-Century England, Ann Arbor, MI, UMI Research Press, 1984, p 3.
40 The disqualification of Le Corbusier's submission for the League of Nations competition in 1927 is one example; *see* S. Giedion, *Space, Time and Architecture*, Cambridge, MA, Harvard University Press; London, Oxford University Press, 1967 (fifth edition), pp 530–36.
41 *See* on that subject S. Braggs and D. Harris, *Sun, Sea and Sand: The Great British Seaside*, Stroud, Tempus, 2006.
42 *See* https://www.dlwp.com/about-us/our-story (accessed 15 December 2018).
43 *See* A. Fairley, *De La Warr Pavilion: The Modernist Masterpiece*, London and New York, Merrell, 2006, p 39.
44 The metal-plated plywood that the Isokon promoted (*see* page 143), and the copper-faced plywood used for the interior transformation of the Finella house by Raymond McGrath (*see* page 143) were materials typically answering the luxurious taste of Art Deco interiors. See A. Powers, *Serge Chermayeff: Designer, Architect, Teacher*, London, RIBA Publications, 2001, pp 37–8.
45 *See* A. Tinniswood, *The Art Deco House: Avant Garde Houses of the 1920s and 1930s*, London, Mitchell Beazley, 2002, pp 6–15.
46 *See* L. Blagojević, *Modernism in Serbia: The Elusive Margins of Belgrade Architecture 1919–1941*, Cambridge, MA, and London, MIT Press, 2003.
47 *See* A. Urrutia Núñez, 'Luis Gutiérrez Soto (1900–1977): arquitectura de los años 20–30', *in* A. Urrutia Núñez, *Arquitectura Española siglo XX*, Madrid, Cátedra, 1997, pp 321–7.
48 *See* 'El Club Náutico de San Sebastián', *AC Documentos de Actividad Contemporánea*, no. 3; A. Urrutia Núñez, 'El Real Club Náutico de San Sebastián (1928–9)', *in* A. Urrutia Núñez, *Arquitectura Española siglo XX*, Madrid, Cátedra, 1997, pp 340–42.
49 *See* Tinniswood, *The Art Deco House*, pp 42–5.
50 Hitchcock, 'Modern Architecture in England', pp 25–41.

AFTERWORD

1 The UIA was founded in Lausanne in 1948.

IMAGE CREDITS

Figure 1.1	Antigoni Katsakou / *DOMUS* vol. 79, no. 12, July 1934, p. 16
Figure 1.2	*DOMUS* vol. 79, no. 12, July 1934, p. 17
Figure 1.3	Dimitris Pikionis Archive / Modern Architecture Archives Benaki Museum
Figure 1.4	Dimitris Pikionis Archive / Modern Architecture Archives Benaki Museum
Figure 1.5	Dimitris Pikionis Archive / Modern Architecture Archives Benaki Museum
Figure 1.6	Dimitris Pikionis Archive / Modern Architecture Archives Benaki Museum
Figure 1.7	Dimitris Pikionis Archive / Modern Architecture Archives Benaki Museum
Figure 1.8	Dimitris Pikionis Archive / Modern Architecture Archives Benaki Museum
Figure 1.9	Bibliothèque Nationale de France
Figure 1.10	Arturo Sicilia / Shutterstock.com
Figure 2.1	Danielle Tinero / RIBA Collections
Figure 2.2	Scala / DACS 2019
Figure 2.3	Amancio Williams Archive / Claudio Williams (dir.)
Figure 2.4	Amancio Williams Archive / Claudio Williams (dir.)
Figure 2.5	Atelier 5 Architekten und Planer
Figure 2.6	Atelier 5 Architekten und Planer
Figure 2.7	FLC / ADAGP / DACS 2019
Figure 2.8	Ezra Stoller / ESTO
Figure 2.9	Andreas Harvik / National Museum Norway
Figure 2.10	Knut Knutsen / National Museum Norway
Figure 2.11	Talette Rørvik Simonsen / National Museum Norway
Figure 2.12	Jens Selmer / Elisabeth Selmer
Figure 2.13	Frøde Larsen / published in E. Tostrup, *The thoughtful architecture of Wenche Selmer*, New York, Princeton Architectural Press, 2006, p. 131
Figure 3.1	Antigoni Katsakou
Figure 3.2	Antigoni Katsakou
Figure 3.3	John Mitchell / Alamy Stock Photo
Figure 3.4	FLC / ADAGP / LCS – Colour Keyboard, Atmosphère 1931
Figure 3.5	Annar Bjørgli / National Museum Norway
Figure 3.6	Alexandra Tsoukala / Dimitris Konstantinidis
Figure 3.7	Alexandra Tsoukala / Dimitris Konstantinidis
Figure 3.8	George Makris
Figure 3.9	Kyriakos Krokos Archive / Modern Architecture Archives Benaki Museum
Figure 3.10	Michalis Souvatzidis
Figure 3.11	Jean Michel Landecy / Stéphane Fernandez
Figure 3.12	Jean Michel Landecy / Stéphane Fernandez
Figure 3.13	Allen Valejo / Legorreta Architects
Figure 4.1	Graphische Sammlung Albertina
Figure 4.2	Lola Alvarez Bravo / Archives of American Art, Smithsonian Institution
Figure 4.3	Antigoni Katsakou
Figure 4.4	Fabio Shoyama (arch.)
Figure 4.5	Luis E. Carranza
Figure 4.6	Instituto Moreira Salles
Figure 4.7	Luis E. Carranza
Figure 4.8	Diane Ghirardo
Figure 4.9	Gio Ponti Archives
Figure 4.10	Gio Ponti Archives
Figure 5.1	Dennis Hance / RIBA Collections
Figure 5.2	RIBA Collections
Figure 5.3	Akademie Der Künste Berlin
Figure 5.4	Akademie Der Künste Berlin
Figure 5.5	Karina Contreras Castellanos (arch.) / Bettina Cetto
Figure 5.6	Karina Contreras Castellanos (arch.) / Bettina Cetto
Figure 5.7	Gio Ponti Archives
Figure 5.8	Antigoni Katsakou / DACS
Figure 5.9	*DOMUS* vol. 380, no. 7, July 1961, p. 38
Figure 5.10	*DOMUS* vol. 380, no. 7, July 1961, p. 36
Figure 5.11	Christ & Gantenbein Architekten
Figure 5.12	Antigoni Katsakou
Figure 6.1	Iliana Miranda-Zacarias
Figure 6.2	Gregori Warchavchik / Carlos Warchavchik
Figure 6.3	Carlos Warchavchik
Figure 6.4	RIBA Collections
Figure 6.5	Karina Contreras Castellanos (arch.)
Figure 6.6	Guillermo Zamora / Archivo Mario Pani
Figure 6.7	Bettina Cetto / Archivo Max Cetto / UAM Azcapotzalco
Figure 7.1	Alan Hastings
Figure 7.2	Architectural Press Archive / RIBA Collections
Figure 7.3	Dell and Wainright / RIBA Collections
Figure 7.4	Architectural Press Archive / RIBA Collections
Figure 7.5	Dell and Wainright / RIBA Collections
Figure 7.6	Dell and Wainright / RIBA Collections
Figure 7.7	Archivo fotográfico del Instituto de Arte Americano e Investigaciones Estéticas "Mario J. Buschiazzo", Facultad de Arquitectura, Diseño y Urbanismo, Universidad de Buenos Aires
Figure 7.8	Architectural Press Archive / RIBA Collections
Figure 7.9	RIBA Collections
Figure 7.10	Architectural Press Archive / RIBA Collections
Figure 7.11	Antigoni Katsakou
Figure 7.12	Antigoni Katsakou
Figure 7.13	*Arhitektura* (Ljubljana) vol. 3, n. 1-2, 1933, p. 20
Figure 7.14	Julian Osley / RIBA Collections
Figure 7.15	Real Canoe Natación Club Madrid
Figure 7.16	*AC Documentos de actividad contemporánea* n. 3, 1931, p. 21
Figure 7.17	*Design in Everyday Things*, British Broadcasting Corporation, 1937, p. XVIII

INDEX

Page numbers in **bold** indicate figures.

Aalto, Alvar 57, 92–93, **93**, 97, 147
Ábalos, Iñaki 26
Africa 169–170
Aizpurúa, José Manuel 162–163, **163**
Albers, Josef 46, 51, 114
Alfaro Siquieros, David 76
Algeria 170
    Oued Ouchaia project 33
Amaral, Tarsila do 118
Ambasz, Emilio 33
Andrade, Mário de 118
Andrade, Oswald de 3, 118
Argentina 112, 113, 114
    Antonio Vilar house, San Isidro, Buenos Aires 150, **150**
    Curutchet House, Buenos Aires 33–34, **34**, 122
    House over the Brook, Buenos Aires 28–30, **29**
    Viviendas en el Espacio project 30–31, **31**, 33, 35
Asplund, Erik Gunnar 155
Atelier 5 31–33, **32**, 35
Austria 115
    Adolf Loos apartment, Vienna 69, **70**
    Goldmann and Salatch building, Vienna 69

Bac, Ferdinand 15, **16**
Bang, Ove 36–38, **37**
Barragán, Luis 13–18, **17**, 46–47, 48–52, **50**, 62, 65, 76, 99, 131, 132, 171
Bawa, Geoffrey 169, 171
Belgium 170
    Hôtel Wolfers, Brussels 62
Blackwell, Ursula 151
Blundell Jones, Peter 57, 69, 99
Bo Bardi, Lina 2, 122–123, 134
Bonet, Antonio 113
Brazil 3, 71, 77–84, 88, 112, 113, 114, 116–124, 134
    Brazilian Press Association building, Rio de Janeiro 121
    Capela da Pampulha, Belo Horizonte 77, **78**, 81
    Casa do Baile, Pampulha, Belo Horizonte 77, **79**
    Glass House, Morumbi, São Paulo 122–123
    João Arnstein House, São Paulo 123–124
    Marjore Prado House, São Paulo 118, 119
    Ministry of Education and Public Health (MESP) building, Rio de Janeiro 81–82, **82**, 84, 121
    Ouro Preto Grande Hotel 81
    Parque Eduardo Guinle, Rio de Janeiro 81
    Rua Barão de Limeira residential building, São Paulo 118–119, **120**
    Rua Itápolis house, Pacaembu, São Paulo 118, **119**
    Sedes Sapientiae Educational Institute, São Paulo 122
    SESC Pompeia cultural centre, São Paulo 122
    Walther Moreira Salles residence, Rio de Janeiro **80**, 81
Breuer, Marcel 143, 147–150, **148**, **149**
Britain 134–135, 138–165, 170
    Broadcasting House, Portland Place, London 158–159
    De La Warr Pavilion, Bexhill-on-Sea 155, 157–159, **157**, 165
    Eltham Palace, Greenwich, London **160**
    Gane exhibition pavilion, Bristol 147, **148**
    Highpoint One, Highgate, London 153, **154**
    Hornsey Town Hall, Crouch End, London 155
    Ideal Home Exhibition, London 142–143, **142**
    Impington Village College, Cambridgeshire 143, 145–146, **145**
    Isokon Building, Hampstead, London 143, **144**
    Kennet House, Manchester 164–165, **164**
    Macnabb House, East Preston, West Sussex 147, 148–150, **149**
    Penguin Pool, London Zoo 153
    Peter Jones store, Sloane Square, London 165
    Richmond Girls' High School, Yorkshire 146–147, **146**
    Royal Corinthian Yacht Club, Burnham-on-Crouch 139
    Serge Chermayeff house, Halland, East Sussex 151, **152**
    Shakespeare Memorial Theatre, Stratford-upon-Avon 155, **156**
    Trellick Tower, London 153
    Venesta Plywood Company exhibition stand, London 142, 143
    Willow Road houses, Hampstead, London 151, 153
Burle Marx, Roberto 81, 121, 122

Caccia Dominioni, Luigi 88
Candela, Felix 76
Cárdenas, Lázaro 124, 125
Carrà, Carlo 3
Carvalho, Flávio de 118
Cetto, Max 76, 99–101, **100**, **101**, 130–132, **133**, 134
Cézanne, Paul 7
Chermayeff, Serge 138, 151, **152**, **157**, 158–159
Chile
    Errazuris House project 58
Chirico, Giorgio de 3, 7
Chomette, Henri 170
Christ & Gantenbein 105, **108**, **109**
Christie, Agatha 143
Clarke Hall, Denis 146–147, **146**
Coates, Wells 138, 143, **144**, 158
Coderch de Sentmenat, José Antonio 103–104, **104**
Colombia 112, 113, 115–116
    Universidad Nacional de Colombia, Bogotá 115
Colquhoun, Alan 92
Costa, Lúcio 3, 81, 114, 116, 121
Croatia 159
    Baćvice Bay, Split, **160**
Cuevas, José Luis 124
Czech Republic
    Tugendhat House, Brno 28

De Cáceres, Rafael 103
De Silva, Minnette 168–169, 171
De Stijl 52, 53, 54–55, 127
Díaz Morales, Ignacio 15
Dobrović, Nicola **160**
Dominioni, Luigi Caccia 105, **106**, **107**
Drew, Jane 138, 169
Dudok, Marinus 55, 155

Eames, Charles 56
Eames, Ray 56
Emberton, Joseph 139
Entwistle, Clive 141, 142–143, **142**, 147

Fehn, Sverre 36, 40
Fernandez, Atelier 62–65, **64**
Ferrari Hardoy, Jorge 113
Figini, Luigi 4
Finland
    Villa Mairea, Noormarkku 92–93, **93**

Forbes, Mansfield 143
Frampton, Kenneth 18
France 159, 170
    La Roche House, Paris 94–95
    Les Graines D'Étoiles nursery, Aix-en-Provence 62–65, **64**
    Maisons Jaoul, Neuilly-sur-Seine 52, 115
    Maisons La Roche-Jeanneret, Paris 53
    Unités d'Habitation, Marseille 128
    Villa Mandrot, Le Pradet 28, 58
    Villa Savoye, Poissy 52, 53, 69, 95–96
    Villa Stein-de-Monzie, Vaucresson 52
Frank, Edward 95
Fraser, Valerie 48, 76
Fry, Maxwell 138, 143, 145–146, **145**, 169

Gaudí, Antoni 159
Germany 115
    Baensch House, Spandau, Berlin **98**
    Bruno Taut house, Dahlewitz, Berlin 97
    R128 House, Stuttgart 27
    Riehl House, Berlin 27–28
    Schocken store, Stuttgart 24, 159
Gibberd, Frederick
    Pullman Court, Streatham Hill, London 153
Goeritz, Mathias 48, 52, 62, 131
Goeritz, Matthias 76
Goldfinger, Ernö 138, 151–153
González Garaño, Alfredo 113
Goodwin, Philip 112
Greece 3, 7–13, 57–62
    Aris Konstantinidis' weekend house, Aegina 59, **59**
    Arts Centre Building, Athens **63**
    Eftaxias weekend house, Attica 59
    Kakrides House, Sykia 59
    Karamanos residence, Athens 9–11, **10**, **11**
    Makris and Kalavritinou holiday house, Aegina **60**
    Pefkakia Primary School, Athens 12, **13**
    Priene Villa 9, **9**
    Rodakis House, Aegina 8, **8**, 11, **14**
    Vettas residence, Filothei, Athens, 60–62, **61**
Gropius, Walter 23, 25, 97, 143, 145–146, **145**, 147
Gundersen, Gunnar S. 56
Gutiérrez Soto, Luis 159–162, **161**, **162**

Häring, Hugo 97
Herzog & De Meuron 88–89
Hitchcock, Henry-Russell 24, 68–69, 71, 94, 112, 139
Honegger, Denis 116
India
    Sarabhai House, Ahmedabad 115
Ireland
    Geragh, Sandycove, Dublin 164
Italy 3–7, 84–88, 115, 170
    Hotel San Michele, Capri 123
    Laporte House, Milan 86
    Nordic Pavilion, Venice 40
    Palazzo Montecatini, Milan **85**, 86
    Torre Rasini, Milan **83**, 84–86
    Via Vigoni 13, Milan 105, **106**, **107**

Villa alla Pompeiana project 4–7, **5**, **6**
Itten, Johannes 46, 51

Japan
   Imperial Hotel, Tokyo 171
   Prada Store, Tokyo 88–89
Johnson, Philip 24, 68–69, 71
Jordan, Robert Furneaux 143

Kahlo, Frida 47, **47**
Kaimi, Julio 8
Kalavritinou, Yota **60**
Kiesler, Friederick 17
Kim, Chung-up 168
Kim, Jong-sung 168
Kim, Swoo-geun 168
Knutsen, Knut 36, 38–40, **38**, **39**
Königsberger, Otto 169
Konstantinidis, Aris 57–59, **59**
Korn, Arthur 143
Korsmo, Arne 36, 55–56, **56**, 62
Korsmo, Grete 56
Krokos, Kyriakos 60–62, **61**
Kurchan, Juan 113

Labayen, Joaquín 162–163, **163**
Lahuerta, José 69–70
Lanza, Emilio **83**, 84–86
Le Corbusier 3, 15, 22–23, 25, 28, 33–34, **34**, 36, 48, 52–54, **54**, 58, 68, 69, 71, 81, 94–96, 113–114, 115, 118, 122, 127–128, 138, 140, 141–143, **142**, 151, 153, 168
Leatherbarrow, David 58
Legorreta, Ricardo 62–65
Levi, Rino 122
Livett, Richard 164–165, **164**
Loos, Adolf 17, 68–71, **70**
Lubetkin, Berthold 153–154, **154**

McGrath, Raymond 158
Makris, George 60, **60**
Marinetti, Tomasso Filippo 3, 114
Mendelsohn, Erich 24, 97, **157**, 158–159
Méndez Rivas, Federico 76
Mérida, Carlos 128
Mexico 13–16, 46–52, 71–77, 88, 112, 114, 116, 124–132, 134
   Acapulco Yacht Club 130, **131**
   Anahuacalli Museum, Mexico City 76
   Camino Real Hotel, Mexico City 62–65, **65**
   Casa Azul, Coyoácan, Mexico City 47, **47**
   Centro Urbano Presidente Alemán, Mexico City 128, **129**, 134
   Centro Urbano Presidente Juárez, Mexico City 128
   Ciudad Universitaria, Mexico City 128
   Cobos House, Veracruz **117**
   Colonia Pro-Hogar primary school, Mexico City **126**
   Corpus Christi project 126–127
   Cristo House, Guadalajara 48
   Gilardi House, Tacubaya, Mexico City 46, 48, 51–52
   González Luna House, Guadalajara 15, **17**
   Juan O'Gorman house, San Ángel, Mexico City 72–73, **74**
   Lomas de Becerra project 125–126
   Luis Barragán house and studio, Tacubaya, Mexico City 46, 48–51, **50**, 62
   Nonoalco-Tlatelolco housing complex, Mexico City 128
   Pedregal housing development, Mexico City 13, 18, 99–101, **100**, **101**, 131–132, 134
   Quintana Weekend House, Tequesquitengo, Morelos 132, **133**
   Reforma Hotel, Mexico City 127
   Rivera Kahlo House, San Ángel, Mexico City 47–48, **49**
   Robles León House, Guadalajara 15
   Secretariat of Hydraulic Resources, Mexico City 130
   University Library, Mexico City 71, 73–76, **75**, 77, 88
Meyer, Hannes 25, 124–127
Mies van der Rohe, Ludwig 25–28, **25**, **27**, 57, 168
Moholy-Nagy, László 143, 151
Mondrian, Piet 53

Montaner, Josep Maria 2
Moral, Enrique del 128, 130
Moralis, Nikos 59
Moses, Herbert 121
Muthesius, Hermann 141

Nervi, Pier Luigi 88
Netherlands
   Café de Unie, Rotterdam 55
   Hilversum Town Hall 155
   Schröder House, Utrecht 55
Neutra, Richard 130, 132, 145
Niemeyer, Oscar 77, **78**, **79**, 81, 116, 121
Norberg-Schulz, Christian 36, 38, 56
Norway 36–43, 55–56
   Knut Knutsen summer cottage, Portø 38–40, **38**, **39**
   Planetveien 12, Oslo 55, 56
   Villa Dammann, Oslo 55, 56, 62
   Villa Stenersen, Oslo 55, **56**
   Villa Stousland II, Sogn, Oslo 36–38, **37**
   Wenche Selmer house, Gråkammen, Oslo 40, **40**, 42

Ocampo, Victoria 113
O'Gorman, Juan 47–48, **49**, 71–76, **74**, **75**, 88, 125, **126**, 127, 131
Orlandos, Anastassios 9, **9**
Orozco, José Clemente 17, 76, 128
Östberg, Ragnar 155
Oud, Jacobus Johannes Pieter 55

Pallasmaa, Juhani 93
Palomar, Juan 48
Pani, Mario 76
Pani Darqui, Mario 127–130, **129**, **131**
Papadaki, Stamo 112
Perret, Auguste 114, 116
Perriand, Charlotte 142, 143
Pevsner, Nikolaus 140–141
Piacentini, Marcello 114, 117
Pikionis, Dimitris 3, 7–13, **8**, **10**, **11**, **13**, **14**, 18, 57, 171
Pizano de Brigard, Francisco 115
Poelzig, Hans 101, 132
Poland 115
   Wolf House, Guben **27**, 28
Pollini, Gino 4
Ponti, Gio 4–7, **5**, **6**, 18, **83**, 84–88, **85**, **87**, 101–103, **102**, 123, 171
Portinari, Cândido 77, **78**, 82, **82**, 84
Pouillon, Fernand 170
Powers, Alan 140
Prebisch, Alberto 114
Pritchard, Jack 143, 158
Pritchard, Molly 143
Pugin, A.W.N. 140

Raymond, Antonin 171
Redig de Campos, Olavo **80**, 81
Reidy, Affonso Eduardo 81
Reiner, Jan 36
Reyes, Chucho 46, 47
Rietveld, Gerrit 55
Rivera, Diego 47, 76
Roberto, Marcelo 121
Roberto, Milton 121
Robertson, Howard 141
Rogers, Ernesto Nathan 71
Rother, Leopold 115
Rudofsky, Bernard 7, 123–124
Rüegg, Arthur 53

Saarinen, Eliel 114
Salmona, Rogelio 115
Samper, Germán 115
Santos, Eduardo 116
Sartoris, Alberto 114
Scharoun, Hans 97, **98**, 103
Scott, Elisabeth 155, **156**

Scott, Michael 164
Scully, Vincent 94
Segarra Tomás, Enrique 116, **117**
Selmer, Jens Andreas 40
Selmer, Wenche 36, 40–42, **40**, **41**
Sert, Josep Lluís 115
Sironi, Mario 3
Slater and Moberly 165
Sobek, Werner 27
South Korea 168
   French Embassy, Seoul 168
   Pusan National University 168
Souvatzidis, Michalis 60, 62, **63**
Spain 115, 159–163
   Barcelona Pavilion 57
   Casa de la Marina, Barceloneta, Barcelona 103
   Cine Barceló, Madrid **161**, 162
   Olano House, Comillas 103–104, **104**
   Piscina La Isla complex, Madrid 162, **162**
   Real Club Náutico, San Sebastián 162–163, **163**
   Ugalde House, Caldes d'Estrac, Barcelona 103
Sri Lanka 168, 169, 171
Sweden 155
   Lerici Italian Cultural Institute, Stockholm 88
   Stockholm City Hall 155
   Stockholm Library 155
Switzerland
   Catholic University, Fribourg 116
   Halen Estate, Bern 31–33, **32**, 35
   Volta Mitte development, Basel 105, **108**, **109**

Tange, Kenzo 168
Taut, Bruno 97
Taut, Max 97
Tecton 153, **154**
Tostrup, Elisabeth 42

United States
   Brazilian Pavilion, New York World´s Fair 121
   Dominus Winery, Napa Valley, California 88–89
   Ennis House, Los Angeles, California 73
   Fallingwater, Bear Run, Pennsylvania 28, 93–94
   Farnsworth House, Plano, Illinois 25, 26–27
   Jacobs House II, Middleton, Wisconsin 35, **35**
   Kahn House, San Francisco 132
   Millard House, Pasadena, California 73
   Robie House, Chicago 95, **96**
Uren, Reginald 155
Uruguay 113
Urzúa Arias, Rafael 15

van de Velde, Henry 62
van Doesburg, Theo 28, 53
Vargas, Getúlio 84, 114, 121
Vasconcelos, José 76
Venezuela 134
   Torre David vertical community, Caracas 134
   Villa Arreaza, Caracas 7, 123
   Villa Planchart, Caracas **87**, 88, 123
Venizelos, Eleftherios 12
Vilar, Antonio **150**
Villagrán García, José 71, 76–77, 127, 130
Violi, Bruno 115–116
Vrieslander, Klaus 8

Warchavchik, Gregori 117–122, **119**, **120**, 134
Williams, Amancio 28–31, **29**, **31**, 33–35, **34**, 42
Wright, Frank Lloyd 28, 35, **35**, 57, 73, 92, 93–94, 95, **96**, 97, 114, 159, 171

Yáñez, Enrique 124, 125
Yorke, F.R.S. 141, 147–150, **148**, **149**

Zachos, Aristotelis 3
Zevi, Bruno 92, 95, 96, 97, 104